American Prisoner of War Camps

In Northern California

American Prisoner of War Camps

in Northern California

Kathy Kirkpatrick

America Through Time®
Adding Color to American History

For Carol

America Through Time is an imprint of Fonthill Media LLC
www.through-time.com
office@through-time.com

Published by Arcadia Publishing by arrangement with Fonthill Media LLC
For all general information, please contact Arcadia Publishing:
Telephone: 843-853-2070
Fax: 843-853-0044
E-mail: sales@arcadiapublishing.com
For customer service and orders:
Toll-Free 1-888-313-2665

www.arcadiapublishing.com

First published 2019

ISBN 978-1-63499-093-6

Typeset in Minion Pro 10pt on 13pt
Printed and bound in England

Contents

List of Illustrations

Introduction

America is a nation of immigrants, so hosting prisoners of war (POWs) from their homelands brought mixed feelings among the civilians and military in the communities where the prisoners were housed and worked. For many farmers who had immigrated to the Midwest, being able to contract for German POW labor not only eased the labor shortage, but it also brought the opportunity to speak their native language, perhaps to learn about family and friends left behind when they immigrated to America. It also often gave them the opportunity to provide additional food for men who worked hard for them and shared their friendship. Although these Americans had sons fighting in the war, they were more aware of the lack of choices these German prisoners had in their own lives than those who had not left an oppressive homeland.

The same situation applied to Italian immigrants and Italian POWs with the additional benefit of a less strained relationship after Italy became a part of the Allied cause in September 1943. The resulting friendships (and some marriages) show the very positive results of their experiences under very difficult circumstances.

In fact, when German-American or Italian-American families were given permission to hire prisoners of war to work on their farms or canneries, they were being given a measure of approval often missing in their own communities. In 1940, 330, 000 Germans and 694,000 Italians had registered as aliens. Those not living on the coasts were not displaced, but suffered the name-calling and ostracism promoted by the government and media directed at those groups of people during that time to promote the war effort. They could be arrested just for translating English into German for an aged grandparent.

From *Una Storia Segreta* by Lawrence Distasi. The licensing metadata from the picture claims that it is a "work prepared by an officer or employee of the United States Government as part of that person's official duties."

The stories shared in the course of researching this topic include a moving description by a young Girl Scout raising the flag near Park City, UT while a truck load of prisoners passed by, with tears in their eyes. Even as a child, she understood that those men deeply loved and missed their children now living in harm's way.

Following the war, some of these farm families corresponded with the former prisoners until their deaths. A treasure trove of about 350 letters and photos from German former prisoners has recently been discovered in a home in Tennessee. They are now housed at the Lipscomb University in Nashville. They met by working on that farm and kept in touch over the years. But it was secret. The letters were found in a cereal box in a closet and even the children of this woman did not know about them.

For many years into the 1970s and 1980s, as late as 2009, there were reunions and family trips made by former prisoners to their old camps and the farms where they worked. They also visited the graves of their comrades who did not survive to go home at the end of the war.

Of the half-million German immigrants arriving here in the United States from 1947-1960, several thousand had spent time here as prisoners of war. The same can be said of Italian immigrants after World War II. They had friends and good experiences here that motivated them to move here themselves.

Even among those enemy aliens who were forced to repatriate at the end of World War II in exchange for Americans and for other reasons, the vast majority had agreed to the arrangement because it guaranteed them the ability to return to the US at a later date. They later used that agreement to return home to the US. That included Germans, Italians, and Japanese.

Prisoners were moved between Service Command areas in 1943 as the US built more camps and received more prisoners from overseas. Later, the prisoners were moved within a Service Command as necessary to provide seasonal labor on farms and in canneries as well as other work necessary for civilians as well as the military population.

Using a variety of sources in the United States and Italy, the complete story will be told. Sources cited include military records now housed at the National Archives II (in College Park, MD), documents from the Italian Army Archives in Rome (aka Stato Maggiore Esercito), L'Ufficio Informazione Vaticano per prigionieri di guerra istituito da Pio XII in the Vatican Secret Archives, as well as many books, articles, websites, and photographs.

Also utilized are interviews with former POWs, guards, translators (and their families) and many other sources both published and unpublished. Their experiences will also be compared to those of German POWs and internees held in America during World War I.

Above: Entrance to the Vatican Secret Archives. [*Photo by author*]

Below: German Prisoners of War at Fort Douglas (UT) in 1917 (crews of German ships). [*Courtesy of Utah Historical Society*]

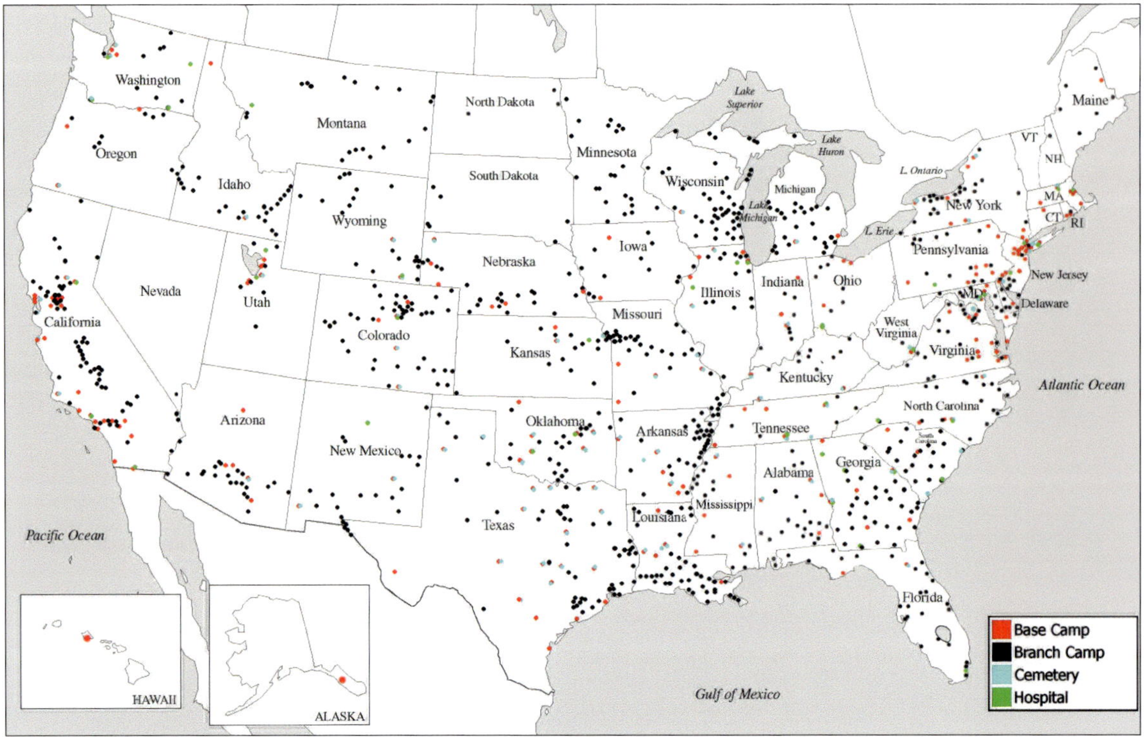

Map of POW Camps and Hospitals Across America. [*Courtesy of John Saffell*]

Background

By the time the US entered World War II (WWII), almost the whole world was at war. This situation included large numbers of POWs which could no longer be supported by the limited resources of the British and French who captured many of them, primarily in North Africa in 1939.

The US had already prepared plans for camps to house large numbers of enemy aliens, so assisting with prisoners captured by the British was easily incorporated into those general plans. It was determined early that the US would not be imprisoning as many enemy aliens as first planned. The number of resident aliens who matched the original enemy alien profile was much larger than anticipated, so implementing that original plan was not possible.

During World War I (WWI), only 1,346 POWs were held on United states soil. They were the crews of German military ships lying in US ports when the war began. They were held in the same five locations as civilian enemy aliens, plus four additional branch locations for a total of 5,887 prisoners of war. All other prisoners of that war captured by the US were held in France.

Those US locations included the following:

War Prison Barracks No. 1: Fort McPherson, East Point, GA: 100 prisoners maximum

War Prison Barracks No. 2: Fort Oglethorpe, Catloosa County, GA: 800 prisoners maximum

War Prison Barracks No. 3: Fort Douglas, Salt Lake City, UT: 406 POWs and 786 enemy aliens.

On 21 March 1918, the POWs were transferred from Fort Douglas to Fort McPherson. On 19 Jul 1919, 108 Conscientious Objectors arrived at Fort Douglas from Fort Leavenworth, KS. They were housed in the compound left vacant by the POWs.

Branch camps under the camps in GA:

Camp Devens, Ayer, MA: 100 prisoners maximum

Camp Grant, Rockford, IL: 100 prisoners maximum

Camp Jackson, Columbia, SC: 100 prisoners maximum

Camp Sevier, Greenville, SC: 100 prisoners maximum

Camp Sherman, near Chillicothe, OH: 100 prisoners maximum

Camp Wadsworth, Spartanburg, SC: 100 prisoners maximum

Left: Monument to German POWs from WWI at Fort Douglas, UT. The US did not separate the Enemy Aliens from the POWs, so only two of the twenty-one men on this list were POWs. [*Photo by author*]

Below: US Service Command Areas map. [*National Archives and Records Administration II in College Park, MD, Record Group 389*]

These camps were run by the Provost Marshal General's Office (PMGO) of the US Army. Initially, there were no distinctions between captured German sailors and enemy aliens rounded up from across the US. However, it soon became apparent that the two groups were quite different, and efforts were made to put different groups into different camps.

Another camp, called an Internment Camp, was established at Hot Springs, NC and run by the Immigration and Naturalization Service (INS). It held 2,200 Germans from commercial ships in US ports when war broke out in 1914. They were placed at Hot Springs in May 1917 for the remainder of the war. Burials from this location were removed to Chattanooga National Cemetery after that war.

Preparing for War

The military headquarters and training for the Ninth Service command moved inland from the Presidio of San Francisco, CA to Fort Douglas, UT at the end of 1941 to make it less vulnerable to a Japanese attack.

The US needed:

1. Labor, since most able-bodied young men were expected in military service and efforts to recruit women into the workforce had only limited success. However, "Rosie the Riveter" became iconic and female pilots as well as clerks (military and civilian), nurses, teachers, and many other occupations gained workers from this effort. Those numbers decreased immediately after the war when the men returned home, but steadily increased as time passed.
2. Supplies for military troops overseas as well as military troops and civilians at home. This included timber, cotton, tobacco, food (planting, harvesting, canning, fishing), clothing, arms and ammunition, and transportation vehicles for land, sea and air.
3. Building and maintenance of new and expanded military installations as well as roads, railways, airfields, dams, and camps for POWs and enemy aliens.

Train at Utah ASF Depot. [*Courtesy of Special Collections Department, Stewart Library, Weber State University*]

Global Situation

POWs held by the British and French were straining their limited supplies, so they needed to be farmed out to other Allied nations (Algeria, Australia, Canada, Egypt, Great Britain, India, Kenya, Libya, the Middle East, South Africa, and the US).

POWs were being held in the various theaters of war, but the numbers were much greater than could be used for supply and support behind combat lines. Great Britain held 23,000 German and 250,000 Italian prisoners in August 1942. Plans were made to transport them to places where their care wouldn't pull men from combat and where their labor could be used to ease shortages caused by men away from home.

Generally, ships carrying supplies and men into the European and Mediterranean theaters of war were used to transport POWs back to America, Canada, Australia, etc. While many POWs worried about getting bombed or torpedoed by their own nations, there were few incidents. The SS Benjamin Contee was torpedoed off the coast of Algeria on 16 August 1943 by German aircraft. The ship proceeded to Bone, to Algiers and then to Gibraltar, where emergency repairs were made, then to New York City, arriving 29 January 1944. The bodies of thirty-six unidentifiable Italian prisoners (900 British-held Italian prisoners had been on this ship before the attack) were removed from the most damaged part of the vessel and buried at Long Island National Cemetery.

The German POW population in the US in May 1942 was only thirty-one with one Japanese POW. There were no Italian POWs here at that time.

The Italian POWs were captured by British, French and American troops between 1939 and 1943 in North Africa and Europe. They first arrived in the US in early 1943 through the New York Port of Embarkation.

For the captured officers and naval crews, interrogation centers were their first stops in America. Fort Hunt, VA was the first of these centers. These interrogators denied torture and criticized the Bush administration when they were honored near Alexandria as part of the US Army's Freedom Team salute program in 2007. The National Park Service (NPS), particularly the George Washington Memorial Parkway which now contains the former Fort Hunt, is interviewing veterans of P.O. Box 1142 (as it was known then) to tell their story. The former interrogators include John Gunther Dean, later a career Foreign Service Officer and ambassador to Denmark, who said, "We did it with a certain amount of respect and justice."[1] George Frenkel, another interrogator, said, "During

Byron Hot Springs (CA) back door, the entrance for the POWs, Joint US Army and US Navy interrogation center. [*Courtesy of Carol A. Jensen, historian at Byron Hot Springs*]

the many interrogations, I never laid hands on anyone."[2] He said, "We extracted information in a battle of the wits, I'm proud to say I never compromised my humanity."[3]

The second interrogation center was Byron Hot Springs CA, also known as P. O. Box 651. Following the example of the British to gain maximum cooperation with excellent living conditions, this center was used primarily for the highest-ranking officers while Fort Hunt was used primarily for naval crews. Information gained at Fort Hunt was also used later in the murder trials of naval POWs accused of murder in the camps.

A third location appearing on the camp lists as restricted listing, the same designation as the two locations above, has recently been exposed as Pine Grove Furnace, NY.

These three centers were run by a combination of Military Intelligence, an agency of the Adjutant General's Office (G-2), and the Office of Naval Intelligence (ONI), so are listed on PMGO lists of POW camps as restricted listing camps.

---

1. Dvorak, Petula, "Fort Hunt's Quiet Men Break Silence on WWII," *Washington Post* (Washington DC: 6 October 2007)
2. Ibid.
3. Ibid.

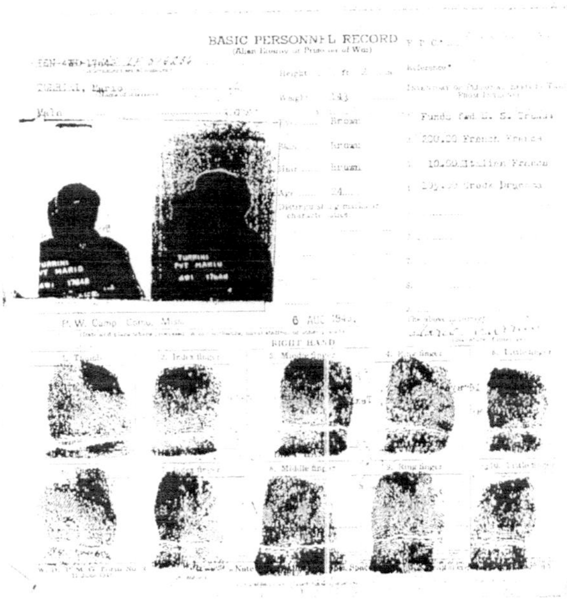

This ID card for Mario Turrini was created at Camp Como, MS. Note that the ID number was crossed out when they realized he already had a POW number assigned by the British who had originally captured him. In the far right column you can see that he had coins from France (from his service in Tunisia), plus coins from Italy (from his Italian Army pay), plus coins from Greece (his last duty station before Tunisia). These documents are courtesy of his son, Marcello, who lives in Italy.

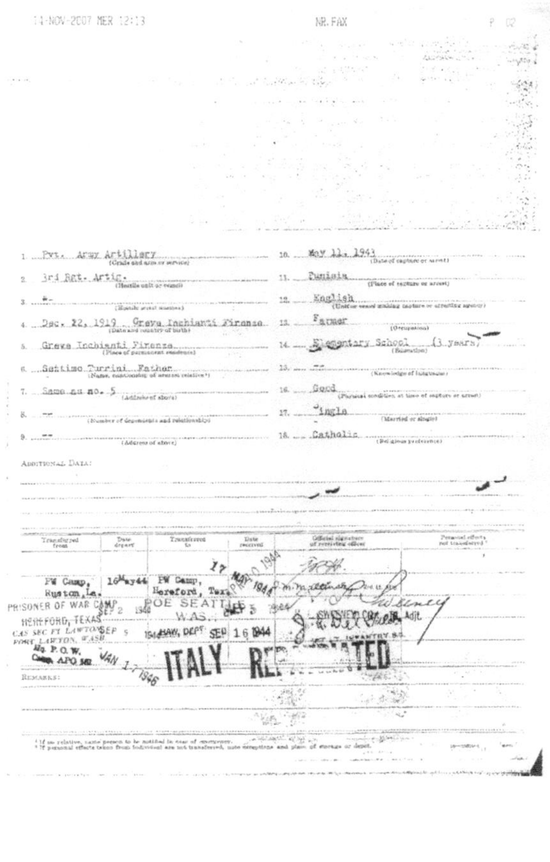
14-NOV-2007 MER 12:13 NR.FAX P. 02

1. Pvt. Army Artillery (Grade and arm or service)
2. 3rd Rgt. Artic. (Hostile unit or vessel)
4. Dec. 22, 1919 Greve Inchianti Firenze (Date and country of birth)
5. Greve Inchianti Firenze (Place of permanent residence)
6. Settimo Turrini Father (Name, relationship of nearest relative)
7. Same as no. 5 (Address of above)
10. May 11, 1943 (Date of capture or arrest)
11. Tunisia (Place of capture or arrest)
12. English
13. Farmer (Occupation)
14. Elementary School (3 years) (Education)
16. Good
17. Single (Married or single)
18. Catholic (Religious preference)

Additional Data:

Transferred from	Date depart	Transferred to	Date received
PW Camp, Ruston, La.	16 May 44	PW Camp, Hereford, Tex.	17 May 1944
Prisoner of War Camp Hereford, Texas	Sep 2 1944	POE Seattle Was.	Sep 5 1944
Cas Sec Ft Lawton Fort Lawton, Wash	Sep 5 1944	Haw. Dept	Sep 16 1944
Hq. P.O.W. Camp APO 962	Jan 17 1946	ITALY REPATRIATED	

Remarks:

This card for Mario Turrini was created at Camp Ruston, LA, his location after processing at Camp Como. It shows that in May 1944 he was transferred to Camp Hereford, TX. This is part of the sorting process and he was categorized as not cooperative since he didn't sign up to be a co-belligerent in the Italian Service Units (ISU) after the fall of Mussolini. In September 1944, he was transferred to the Seattle Port of Entry, particularly Fort Lawton from which he sailed two weeks later for duty at POW Camp APO 950, AKA Fort Armstrong, Honolulu, HI. The Italian prisoners weren't sure where they were going and there was unrest among the African-American units at Fort Lawton, so when one of the Italians committed suicide, three African-American soldiers were convicted of murder. They were finally cleared in 2005, primarily because of the excellent research proving their innocence in *On American Soil* by Jack Hamman.

Planning and Building the Camps

Initially, enemy alien camps were planned for 100,000 internees. However, after it was determined that original parameters for designating enemy aliens as potential threats were too broad and couldn't be implemented because of the vast numbers of people involved, the camps under construction were re-purposed as POW camps. They expected to fill them with POWs already captured by the British, about 100,000.

Lessons learned in WWI led to the separation of POWs (run by the PMGO of the Army) and Enemy Aliens (run by INS within the Department of Justice (DOJ). Also in the wake of WWI were the agreements made at the Geneva Convention in 1929. It was determined that the US would (usually) follow such agreements not only because of the legal obligations, but also in hopes of reciprocal treatment by our enemies.

Among those soldiers captured in German uniform were men who considered themselves another nationality, such as Austrian, Czech, Swiss, Italian, Russian, Mongol, Hungarian, Romanian, and more. Among those captured in Japanese uniform were Koreans. Among those captured in Italian uniforms were Slavs (present day Croatia, Bosnia and Slovenia), Albanians, and Ethiopians. It was quickly learned that these groups needed to be separated in the POW camps both at home and abroad. In many of these groups were those who claimed US citizenship.

One of the POW camps had previously been used as WWI POW camp: Fort Douglas, UT. Some were already military installations, like Fort Jay, NY. Some were former Civilian Conservation Corps (CCC) camps, like Fort Hunt, VA. Many were new purchases, like Camp Monticello, AR.

There were several potential standard plans, adapted to different climates and geographical considerations, but ultimately, each camp was unique in its layout due to geography and transportation infrastructure. In addition to building barracks, mess halls, warehouses, administrative buildings, and a hospital, the first commanding officer of the Utah ASF Depot POW camp, UT designated fifty acres nearby to grow crops to help feed the POWs. The crop yield was so bountiful it was shared with the Depot cafeteria, the Depot quartermaster, Bushnell General Hospital (in Brigham City), and the Ogden Air Service Command at nearby Hill Field. A similar assortment of buildings and garden area was described at other locations.

Above: Garden at Utah ASF Depot [*Courtesy of Special Collections Department, Stewart Library, Weber State University*]

Below: Italian Prisoners of War in freight yard at Utah ASF Depot. [*Courtesy of Special Collections Department, Stewart Library, Weber State University*]

Managing the Camps

Security was a primary concern. Guards were a combination of military (often older men and wounded combat veterans) and civilian. Sometimes long-lasting friendships developed between the guards and the POWs they watched, particularly among the interpreters.

In a successful effort to conserve manpower, it was the experience at Utah ASF Depot, UT that one woman with a dog could patrol the same area as two men.

The POW work details were supervised by guards armed with carbines and rifles. Originally, the ratio was one guard to ten POWs, but over time diminished to one guard to thirty-two prisoners. When American army personnel weren't available, the commander could supply guards from other sources. Handcuffing or abuse was forbidden. Each of the guard towers in the compound was occupied by a guard equipped with machine guns.

Sometimes the US Army translators were also guards, like Thomas M. Todaro, who worked at Camp Monticello and later at Fort Leonard Wood, MO. Translators (usually US Military) were assigned to camps. However, US military translators for Italian Service Units (ISU) were assigned to the units which moved from camp to camp as needed to provide services.

The POWs were soon discovered to be an uneasy (sometimes dangerous) mix of several nationalities, languages, and ideologies—regardless of their uniform. They were then segregated by nationality and politics and rank. In many camps, the officers were simply held in a separate compound from the enlisted, as directed by the Geneva Convention. However, compounds at Camps Beale, Blanding, McCain and Papago Park were designated for German Naval crews. Camp Alva was for Nazis. Camps Blanding, Campbell and Devens, were anti-Nazi camps. Camps Hereford, Monticello, and Weingarten were for Italian Fascists. These divisions into Nazi and anti-Nazi were based on judgments made by G-2, the Army Intelligence unit.

The generalities do not take into account transfers from camp to camp that were frequent and based on additional factors, such as work, health, and relationships. Most POWs didn't accurately fall into the above categories, they were young men who grew up in societies with mandatory youth groups and mandatory military service whose families were living in Nazi controlled locations. After initial interrogation, the German generals were placed at camps Clinton and Dermott while Italian generals and officers were at Camp Monticello. Additional German officers were held at Crossville.

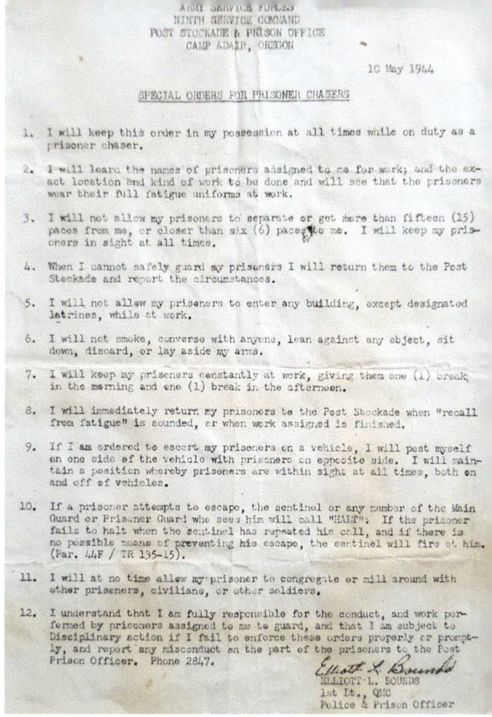

ARMY SERVICE FORCES
NINTH SERVICE COMMAND
POST STOCKADE & PRISON OFFICE
CAMP ADAIR, OREGON

10 May 1944

SPECIAL ORDERS FOR PRISONER CHASERS

1. I will keep this order in my possession at all times while on duty as a prisoner chaser.

2. I will learn the names of prisoners assigned to me for work; and the exact location and kind of work to be done and will see that the prisoners wear their full fatigue uniforms at work.

3. I will not allow my prisoners to separate or get more than fifteen (15) paces from me, or closer than six (6) paces to me. I will keep my prisoners in sight at all times.

4. When I cannot safely guard my prisoners I will return them to the Post Stockade and report the circumstances.

5. I will not allow my prisoners to enter any building, except designated latrines, while at work.

6. I will not smoke, converse with anyone, lean against any object, sit down, discard, or lay aside my arms.

7. I will keep my prisoners constantly at work, giving them one (1) break in the morning and one (1) break in the afternoon.

8. I will immediately return my prisoners to the Post Stockade when "recall from fatigue" is sounded, or when work assigned is finished.

9. If I am ordered to escort my prisoners on a vehicle, I will post myself on one side of the vehicle with prisoners on opposite side. I will maintain a position whereby prisoners are within sight at all times, both on and off of vehicles.

10. If a prisoner attempts to escape, the sentinel or any member of the Main Guard or Prisoner Guard who sees him will call "HALT". If the prisoner fails to halt when the sentinel has repeated his call, and if there is no possible means of preventing his escape, the sentinel will fire at him. (Par. 44F / TR 135-15).

11. I will at no time allow my prisoner to congregate or mill around with other prisoners, civilians, or other soldiers.

12. I understand that I am fully responsible for the conduct, and work performed by prisoners assigned to me to guard, and that I am subject to Disciplinary action if I fail to enforce these orders properly or promptly, and report any misconduct on the part of the prisoners to the Post Prison Officer. Phone 2847.

Elliott L. Bounds
ELLIOTT L. BOUNDS
1st Lt., QMC
Police & Prison Officer

Above left: POW Farm labor with guards. [*Courtesy of Gary Reeves collection of POW artifacts*]

Above right: Instructions for POW guards, issued at Camp Adair (OR). *Courtesy of Gary Reeves collection of POW artifacts*]

Below left: This British Issue Dog Tag for an Italian enlisted POW was on display at the March Air Field Museum display on Camp Haan (CA). [*Photo by author*]

Below: Thomas M. Todaro, guard and translator. [*Courtesy of his son, Robert*]

Above: Board at Fort Devons (MA) showing those POWs who could work without a guard. [*Courtesy of Gary Reeves collection of POW artifacts*]

Left: Orazio and Angelo Vecchio, brothers and Italian Prisoners at Utah ASF Depot. [*Courtesy of Orazio's grandson, Orazio Vecchio, living in Italy*]

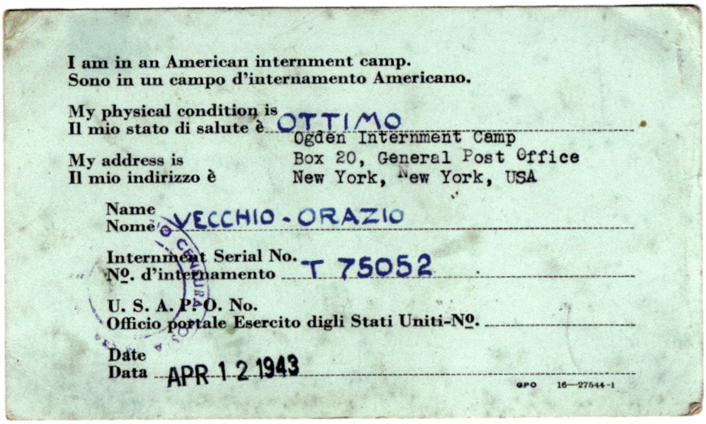

I am in an American internment camp.
Sono in un campo d'internamento Americano.

My physical condition is
Il mio stato di salute è OTTIMO

My address is Ogden Internment Camp
Il mio indirizzo è Box 20, General Post Office
New York, New York, USA

Name
Nome VECCHIO - ORAZIO

Internment Serial No.
No. d'internamento T 75052

U. S. A. P. O. No.
Officio postale Esercito digli Stati Uniti-No.

Date
Data APR 1 2 1943

GPO 16—27544-1

Standard POW form, filled out for Orazio Vecchio. [*Courtesy of his grandson, Orazio Vecchio*]

G-2 interviewed these officers, however the highest-ranking officer in these interrogation teams was a major, so not qualified to deal with an officer of higher rank. Consequently, cursory and sometimes erroneous conclusions were drawn, heavily influenced by other high-ranking officers who were invited to participate.

A glaring example is the input of Italian General Trezzani who used the opportunity to cast doubt (and worse, calling another General a Nazi). He used this ploy on officers of similar rank to promote himself with the Americans. He used it to great advantage to become the head of the Italian Service Units (ISU) in the US and later in charge of rebuilding the Italian Army in post-war Italy.

Additionally, Italian Royalists and career army were considered Fascist while German career army were consider Nazi, simply for participating in required youth groups or in support of Franco (military service) in Spain. There was so much more to the story.

Public opinion was most loudly expressed by those with the greatest fear of enemy camps in their towns, or by those who hoped to profit from the use of POW labor in their businesses. Most Americans viewed the new camps with caution, but acceptance, and gradually came to appreciate the additional civilian jobs and affordable labor source. Some even developed friendships which lasted long after the war ended.

Each prisoner was processed either when captured or when they arrived in the US. This process included searching, delousing, disinfecting, fumigation, bathing, registration, clothing issue, quartering, and medical inspection.

Above left: Giovanni D'Onofrio (third from left) and POW friends at Utah ASF Depot. [*Courtesy of his children, Vincent, Orazio, and Janice*]

Above right: Carlo Selmi and POW friends at Utah ASF Depot. [*Courtesy of his son, Andrea, living in Italy*]

Life in the Camps

The maximum number of German POWs held in the continental US was 371,683 in May 1945. Italian POWs (continental US) reached a maximum of 51,156 in November 1944. Japanese POWs (continental US) reached a maximum of 5,413 in August 1945. There were POW camps in every state except Vermont, plus the territories of Hawaii and Alaska.

The POWs were placed into companies of 250 men each, eight companies to a compound (2,000 men), with two compounds at Ogden ASF Depot in 1943. Later, one compound at Ogden ASF Depot was composed of Italian Service Units while the other housed German POWs who were willing to work there. They were the first camp to work the two groups together, with Germans supervising Italians and the opposite.

Each base camp had a station hospital, staffed by both Americans and POWs. Utah ASF Depot station hospital had 100 beds. Since many POWs arrived in poor health due to long imprisonment and poor diet (both before and after imprisonment), that hospital admitted over 2,000 men by June 1944 after opening only eighteen months earlier.

Housing and furnishings at first met, and then exceeded the Geneva Convention requirements. Since the camps were in different locations, some utilized barracks, some hutments (smaller housing units) while the temporary and seasonal camps often used tents. The Geneva Convention required mattresses only for officers. Eventually, most permanent camps had mattresses, pillows and pillow cases on iron and wooden beds for enlisted men as well as officers.

General Hospitals, run by the Surgeon General of Army Service Forces (ASF), were in each region, utilizing a POW wing to facilitate security. In 1944, they became more specialized to receive all patients from theaters of operations, plus patients needing specialized treatment in the Zone of Interior.

Those station hospitals with airfields were overseen by the Air Surgeon of the Army Air Force (AAF). In 1944, Regional Hospitals (a new designation), station hospitals, and convalescent centers were now run by both the ASF and AAF. The Regional Hospitals were to serve as General Hospitals for Zone of Interior patients. These designations are rarely mentioned in the population lists in the National Archives.

The station hospitals were generally staffed with an American officer of the Medical Corps and three POW attendants with medical training. The surgical staff included an American Medical Officer, a nurse, an enlisted man, and three POW attendants with medical training. POWs also served as lab technicians. The hospital mess was under the mess officer with a civilian nurse and a mess sergeant. It was staffed by two army mess sergeants, one POW mess sergeant and four POW cooks. Provisions were made for special diets.

Mental patients in Washington, Oregon, Idaho, and Utah were sent to Bushnell General Hospital, UT while extreme cases were sent to Mason General Hospital, NY. Dental care was also provided at the station hospital for the POWs treating abscesses, and doing extractions, fillings, and gum treatments. At Utah ASF Depot, over 17,000 dental cases were treated during the year of 1943-1944.

Upon arrival, the POWs were issued clothing and blankets which were maintained and replaced as needed. The Red Cross in New York issued two pairs of blankets per man and a uniform that might be the dark blue with white PW lettering, or an old US Army uniform, plus the uniform he arrived wearing. Not many had overcoats, but some came with English overcoats, which were black with a black diamond on the back.

The POWs were supposed to be adequately, comfortably, and properly clothed in accordance with the climate conditions in which they lived and worked. The War Department later determined that dark blue was a preferable color since it would not be mistaken for the American khaki. They were also provided with woolen underwear, cotton underwear, woolen socks and cotton socks, woolen shirts and cotton shirts, two pairs of trousers in either wool or denim, two coats in wool or cotton, a wool overcoat, a raincoat, woolen caps and hats, cotton hats and caps, shoes and overshoes, gloves, and two heavy woolen blankets. When an item wore out, it was immediately replaced. The clothing was class X or class B, American issue.

Some camps had laundry facilities with machines while some had wash rooms where laundry was done by hand.

Education included language classes, history classes and clerical and equipment training. Supplies were provided for many art projects and newsletter production.

Newspapers were produced by the prisoners at most of the larger camps. There is a collection of Italian POW newsletters at Utah State University. There is a large collection of German POW newsletters at the Library of Congress. Many of these newsletters can be found at local colleges and historical societies.

Their food was the equivalent of that issued to American servicemen (type A field ration), according to the Geneva Convention, although substitutions were made to recognize ethnic preferences. The Italian POWs had an increase in rice, spaghetti, macaroni, noodles and pasta with decreases in meats and baked beans. Germans had an increase in potatoes and a decrease in beans. Meals were served three times daily. Special menus were prepared on Thanksgiving, Christmas, New Year's and other holidays. For many prisoners, these rations exceeded their military experience. The average prisoner at Utah ASF Depot gained fifteen pounds.

The POWs were their own cooks and bakers, paid the same wage as those working in all occupations both in and outside of the camps. However, each camp commander had some autonomy and after the liberation of concentration camps in Germany, some camps restricted food allowances for POWs well below Geneva Convention. Hereford, TX is infamous for its dietary cuts in 1945.

Utah ASF Depot Hospital grounds. [*Courtesy of Special Collections Department, Stewart Library, Weber State University*]

Above left: Utah ASF Depot Hospital steps. [*Courtesy of Special Collections Department, Stewart Library, Weber State University*]

Above right: Utah ASF Depot POW Class with civilian instructor and US Army guard. [*Courtesy of Special Collections Department, Stewart Library, Weber State University*]

POW Oase

LAGERZEITUNG DES KRIEGSGEFANGENEN-LAGERS FORT MCCLELLAN, ALABAMA, U.S.A.

Folge 74

1. Juli 1945

ZUR LAGERCHRONIK

POW Newspaper from Fort McClellan, AL. [*Courtesy of Gary Reeves collection of POW artifacts*]

Some beautiful art was created in the camps, this piece from Colorado shows a sense of humor as well. [*Courtesy of Gary Reeves collection of POW artifacts*]

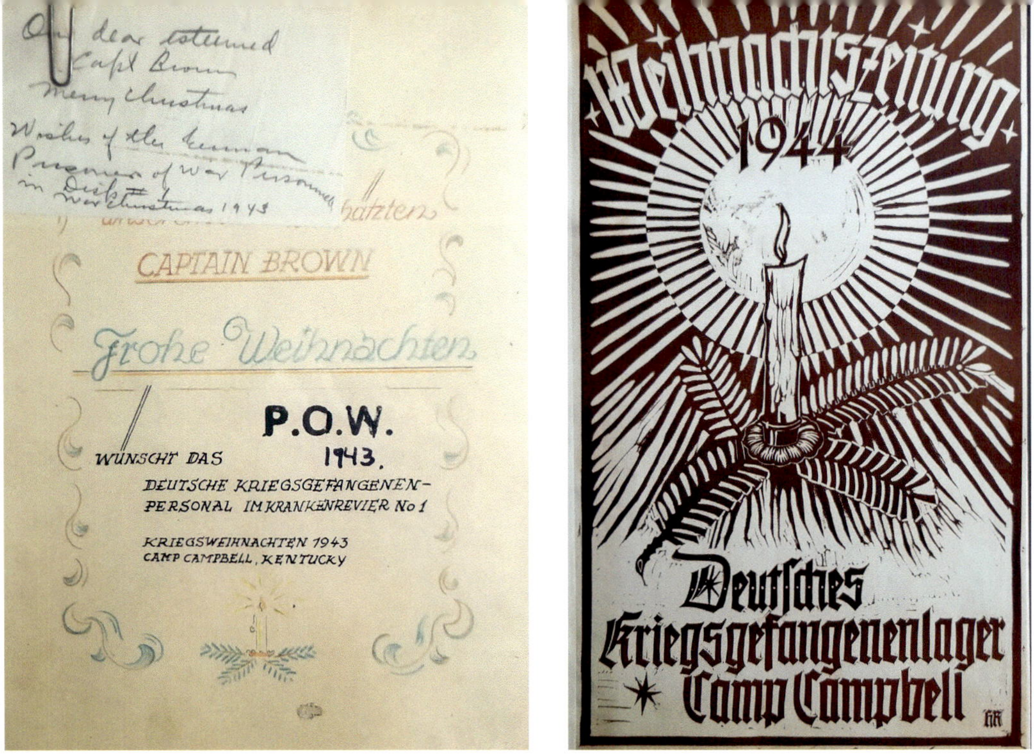

Christmas card from a German POW at Camp Campbell (KY). [*Courtesy of Gary Reeves collection of POW artifacts*]

Italian POW cooks at Utah ASF Depot. [*Courtesy of Special Collections Department, Stewart Library, Weber State University*]

Utah ASF Depot Italian POW Bakery. [*Courtesy of Special Collections Department, Stewart Library, Weber State University*]

Many services were available for POWs, some in accord with the Geneva Convention and some additional benefits. They included Canteens, camp stores where a POW could spend the pay (in coupons) he'd earned working on such items as beer, cigarettes, and gold jewelry (high quality necklaces, wedding rings and rosaries were in high demand by the Italian POWs at Utah ASF Depot). The profits from the sales were returned to the POWs in the form of free beer, cigarettes, and theater tickets.

Some POW photos show the decorations (pin-ups) in their personal areas. These could include small pictures of national leaders and flags and emblems, but large displays were limited to funerals and religious services.

Recreation supplies were provided for many sports, although soccer was most popular. Other equipment included baseball, softball, basketball, football, boxing, volleyball, croquet, horse shoes, badminton, and table tennis. Many game sets were also provided for the POWs including dominoes, Chinese checkers, checkers, backgammon, India, bingo, chess, playing cards, etc. The POWs often constructed their own volleyball courts, baseball diamonds and soccer fields.

POW contacts with families and others included inspection visits from the Red Cross, YMCA, Vatican City, Swiss government, and other welfare organizations. Each POW was permitted two letters and one post card per week, written in ink (not pencil). Also, when necessary, one business letter per week. Special stationary was provided, so limited to the lines on the forms. Free mailing was applied to all letters, postcards, and parcels less than four pounds, addressed to or sent by a

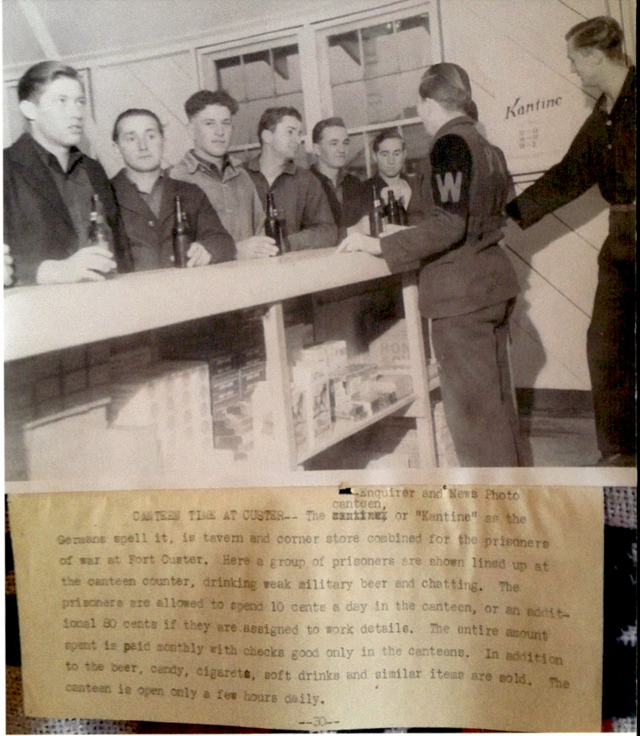

Above left: Ration coupons were issued by each camp, but the format was standardized as shown here of coupons from Camp Livingston (LA), Camp Grant (IL), and Camp Rupert (ID). [*Courtesy of Gary Reeves collection of POW artifacts*]

Above right: This photo was taken for a news service of the Canteen at Camp Custer (MI). [*Courtesy of Gary Reeves collection of POW artifacts*]

Below left: Matchbooks were made for Fort Robinson (NE) and many other camps. [*Courtesy of Gary Reeves collection of POW artifacts*]

Below right: Some camps issued cards for special items, like this Beer Card. [*Courtesy of Gary Reeves collection of POW artifacts*]

Above left: Of course, men create art out of whatever is available, as evidenced by this water canteen with inscriptions from this German soldier's time in Africa in 1943. [*Courtesy of Gary Reeves collection of POW artifacts*]

Above right: These photos of theatrical productions at Edgewood Arsenal (MD) come with comments. [*Courtesy of Gary Reeves collection of POW artifacts*]

Below left: Barracks at Camp Atterbury (IN). [Courtesy of Alessandro de Gaetano]

Below right: POW Soccer Team at Edgewood Arsenal (MD). [*Courtesy of Gary Reeves collection of POW artifacts*]

POW through the US Postal Service. Each POW was also allowed, at his own expense, one prepaid cable or telegram per month. In the event of a serious emergency such as death or serious illness, and at the discretion of the base commander, more than one per month may be sent.

Incoming mail for Italian POWs from relatives in the US was enormous. In two or three months alone, from 300-500 packages were received at Utah ASF Depot. The POWs sent many gifts to their relatives in this country and to those outside the continental US. Correspondence to POWs was permitted from anyone. However, POWs could only write to and receive packages from family members such as wives, grandparents, parents, siblings, aunts, uncles, children, nieces, and nephews.

Most camps had bands or orchestras made up of their POW population. At Ogden, UT, concerts were held once a week. The orchestra also played for stage shows and gave monthly concerts. Many instruments were provided by the Catholic church, others were loaned by the depot quartermaster. At some camps, the local schools and communities provided instruments.

The ISU band played for dances each week, both at the camp at St. Joseph's Catholic Church in Ogden. The dances were a good place to meet the local girls. The POWs were taken to the church by bus from the camp. Separate dances were held on different nights for officers and enlisted POWs to adhere to Geneva Convention.

Religion was also a part of camp life. At first, religious services at Ogden, UT were held in the open with an improvised pulpit. Later, a recreation hall was used part time for morning Mass. An empty barrack was utilized as a regular chapel for weekdays. Later, the old Compound One Headquarters building became the Main Chapel and accommodated about 300 POWs for daily Mass. When Compound Two was activated, one of its recreational halls was provided for chapel functions and accommodated about 700. This camp was Italian, so only Catholic services were required. The hospital also held Mass on Sunday. When the camp opened a German compound, a Lutheran minister provided services on Sunday in addition to the Catholic services for the German POWs.

While POWs weren't allowed to donate blood (prohibited by the PMGO and Geneva Convention), they were allowed to make voluntary contributions to specific organizations, such as the Red Cross and the YMCA. A minor political group at Utah ASF Depot, the Republicans, collected $80 for war bonds and offered to donate blood. and offered the money to the Infantile Paralysis Fund because they believed it was a good cause.

Escapes were expected and did occur at several locations. Most of them were short in duration and distance, usually ending with an easy capture or surrender since the object was just to get outside the fence for a while. Some were more serious, with bigger plans and groups of men, also usually ending in surrender. Just a couple of men were able to remain at large until many years after the war ended. No reports of sabotage or terrorism were ever associated with these escapes.

The most interesting was eleven attempted escapes in the first week of May 1945 at Boswell Ranch in Corcoran, CA. They totaled twenty prisoners, one of whom made three attempts in this time. The most successful attempt was on 3 January when three men scaled the fence amid bullets from the guards. A fourth escaped a few hours later. All four men turned themselves in

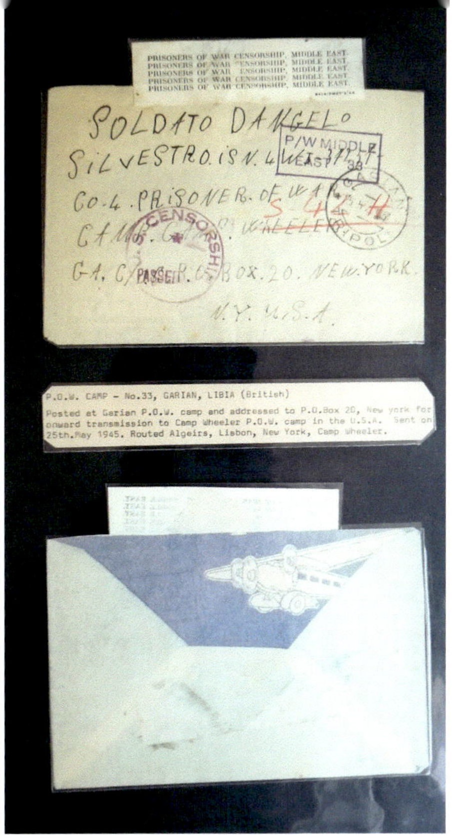

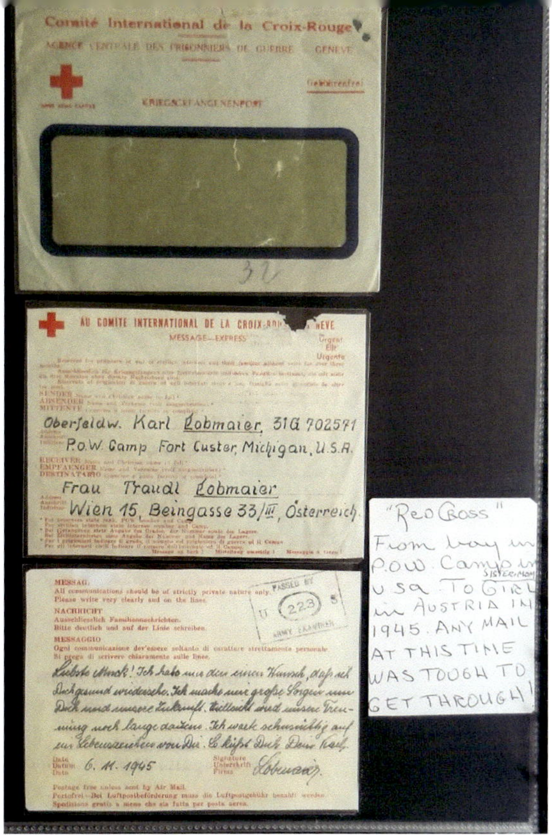

Above left: This letter was sent from a British POW camp in Garian (Libya) to a POW in Camp Wheeler, GA. [*Courtesy of Gary Reeves collection of POW artifacts*]

Above right: This letter was sent through the Red Cross from POW Camp Custer (MI) to a young woman in Austria. Some letters were also sent through the Vatican as an alternative to the US mail. [*Artifact courtesy of Gary Reeves collection of POW artifacts*]

Below: This postcard was designed by a German POW and printed by the YMCA. [*Courtesy of Gary Reeves collection of POW artifacts*]

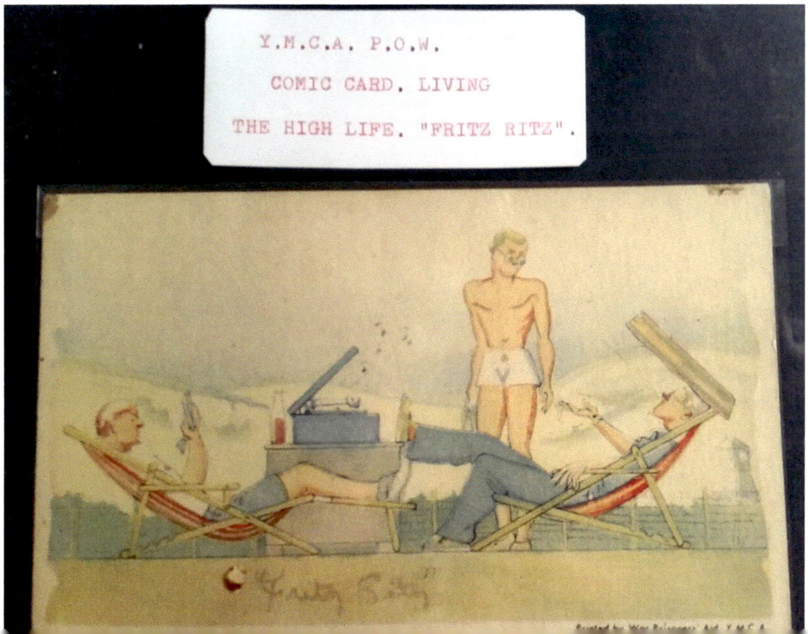

Above left: Postcard with a group photo of German POWs. [*Courtesy of Gary Reeves collection of POW artifacts*]

Above right: Many camps and military installations had their own Postcards. [*Courtesy of Robert Todaro from his father's duty assignment there as a POW translator and guard*]

Postcards with a group photo of German POWs from Camp Swift (TX). [*Courtesy of Gary Reeves collection of POW artifacts*]

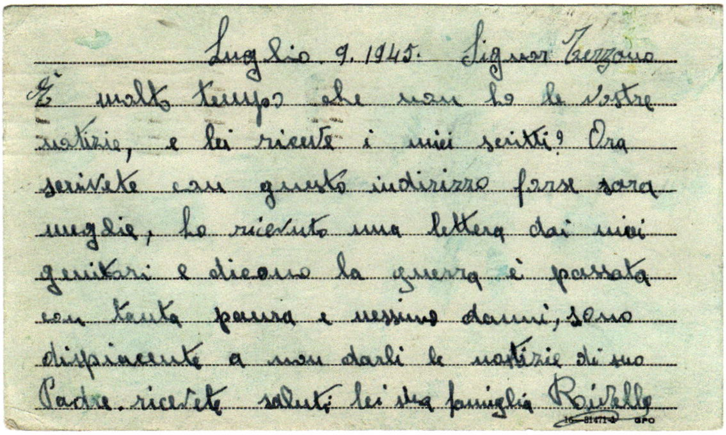
Luglio 9. 1945. Signor Terzano
E' molto tempo che non ho le vostre notizie, e lei ricevute i miei scritti? Ora scrivete con questo indirizzo forse sarà meglio, ho ricevuto una lettera dai miei genitori e dicono la guerra è passata con tanta paura e nessun danni, sono dispiacente a non darli le notizie di suo Padre. ricevete saluti lei sua famiglia Rivella
16—81471-1 GPO

POW Postcard from Fort Douglas (UT).
[*Courtesy of Dennis H. Pack*]

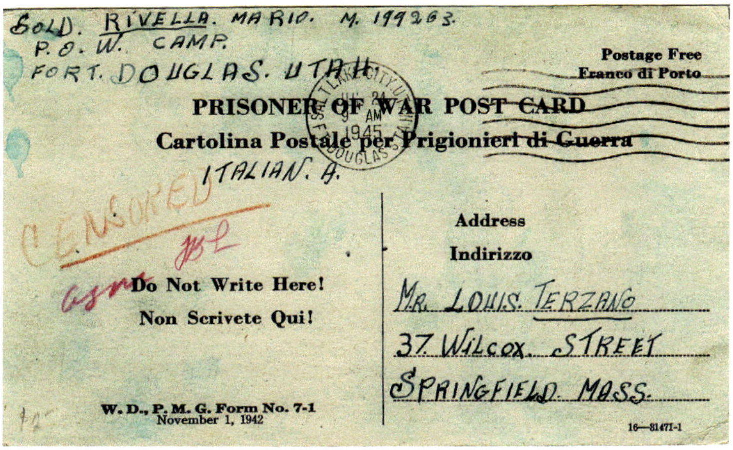
SOLD. RIVELLA. MARIO. M. 199263.
P.O.W. CAMP.
FORT. DOUGLAS. UTAH.
Postage Free
Franco di Porto
PRISONER OF WAR POST CARD
Cartolina Postale per Prigionieri di Guerra
ITALIAN. A.
CENSORED
Do Not Write Here!
Non Scrivete Qui!
Address
Indirizzo
MR. LOUIS. TERZANO
37 WILCOX. STREET
SPRINGFIELD. MASS.
W. D., P. M. G. Form No. 7-1
November 1, 1942
16—81471-1

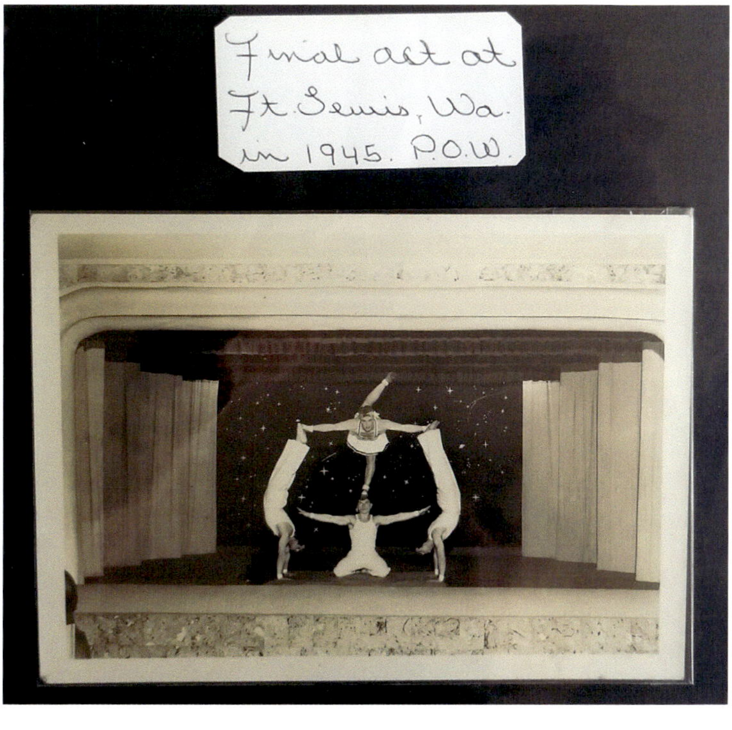

Acrobats on stage at Fort Lewis (WA).
[*Courtesy of Gary Reeves collection of POW artifacts*]

Above: ISU Band at Utah USF Depot. [*Courtesy of Andrea Selmi, son of Carlo Selmi, clarinet player in this band (third from left), living in Italy*]

Below left: This Bible seems to have gone from Win Ferguson to Italian Lt. Sergei Bolasco after being presented by a US Army Chaplain who served at both Fort Riley (KS) and POW Camp Weingarten (MO). [*Courtesy of Gary Reeves collection of POW artifacts*]

Below right: Madonna made and placed at Camp Lockett (CA) near their housing area by Italian POWs. [*Courtesy of Mountain Empire Historical Society*]

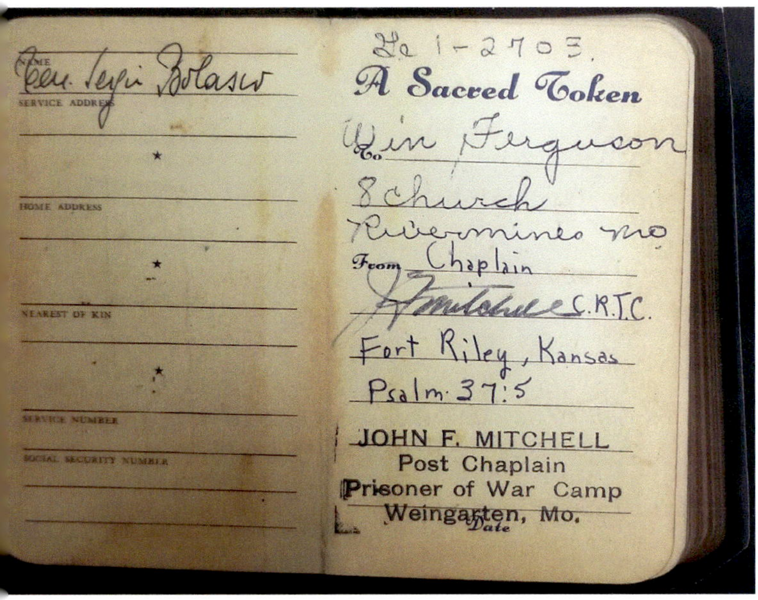

NAME

SERVICE ADDRESS

HOME ADDRESS

NEAREST OF KIN

SERVICE NUMBER

SOCIAL SECURITY NUMBER

A Sacred Token

To Win Ferguson

8 church

From Chaplain

C.R.T.C.

Fort Riley, Kansas

Psalm 37:5

JOHN F. MITCHELL
Post Chaplain
Prisoner of War Camp
Weingarten, Mo.

Date

at the La Hacienda Ranch, twenty miles away, only three days later. The foreman there called the Sheriff to collect the POWs.

There were pets among the POWs, sometimes traveling with them from camp to camp.

POW work included occupations required for the maintenance of the camps, such as cooking, cleaning, clothing and shoe repairs, landscaping, etc.

They also were hired out for canning and farming in the community, including pruning orchards and planting as well as harvesting. They also worked on dams, railroads, orchards, mining, quarrying, and forestry. The businesses and farmers paid the government a minimum wage and the POWs were paid $0.80 a day, comparable to the wage for a civilian day laborer.

Even the Ogden Chamber of Commerce hired POWs. And Italian POWs at Fort Monmouth, NJ were making violins.

Other POWs were working on occupations labeled military, such as at hospitals, supply offices, post exchanges, construction, dying uniforms, landscaping, and woodworking.

A group of Italian POWs at Camp Lockett, CA pose with their priest and their dog. [*Courtesy of Mountain Empire Historical Society*]

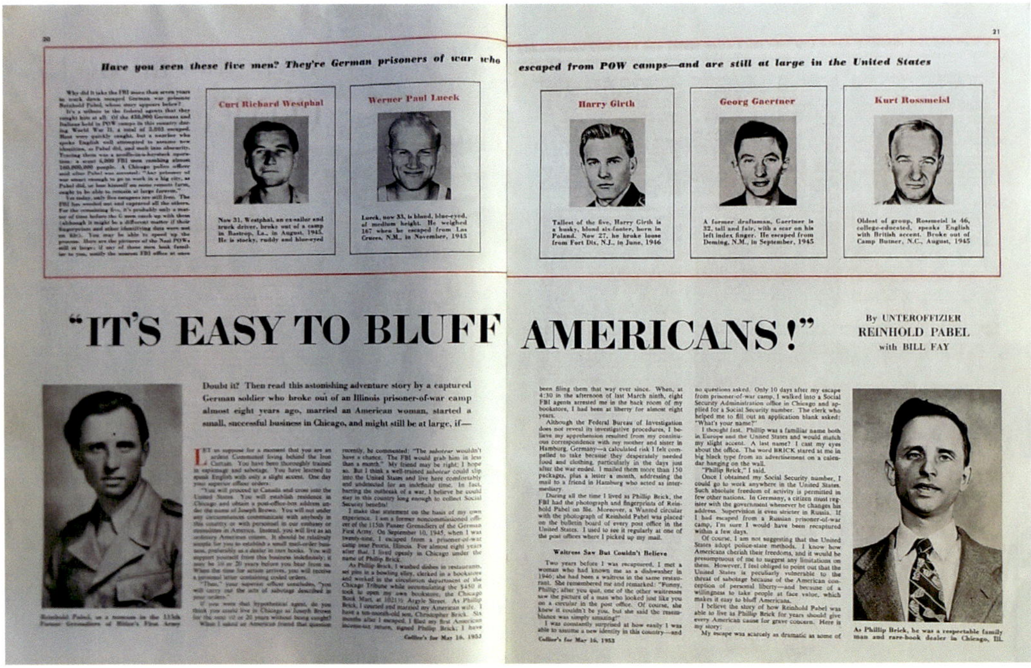
Have you seen these five men? They're German prisoners of war who escaped from POW camps—and are still at large in the United States

Curt Richard Westphal

Now 31, Westphal, an ex-sailor and truck driver, broke out of a camp in Bastrop, La., in August, 1945. He is stocky, ruddy and blue-eyed

Werner Paul Lueck

Lueck, now 33, is blond, blue-eyed, of medium height. He weighed 167 when he escaped from Las Cruces, N.M., in November, 1945

Harry Girth

Tallest of the five, Harry Girth is a husky, blond six-footer, born in Poland. Now 27, he broke loose from Fort Dix, N.J., in June, 1946

Georg Gaertner

A former draftsman, Gaertner is 32, tall and fair, with a scar on his left index finger. He escaped from Deming, N.M., in September, 1945

Kurt Rossmeisl

Oldest of group, Rossmeisl is 46, college-educated, speaks English with British accent. Broke out of Camp Butner, N.C., August, 1945

"IT'S EASY TO BLUFF AMERICANS!"

By UNTEROFFIZIER REINHOLD PABEL with BILL FAY

Doubt it? Then read this astonishing adventure story by a captured German soldier who broke out of an Illinois prisoner-of-war camp almost eight years ago, married an American woman, started a small, successful business in Chicago, and might still be at large, if—

As Phillip Brick, he was a respectable family man and rare-book dealer in Chicago, Ill.

In 1953, Colliers Magazine published a story about five German POW still missing. One escaped from near Bastrop (LA), one from Las Cruces (NM), one from Fort Dix (NJ), one from Deming (NM) and one from Camp Butner (NC). [*Courtesy of Gary Reeves collection of POW artifacts*]

Sometimes POWs worked on community service projects outside the camp. The Catholic Church of St. Mary's in Umbarger, TX was beautifully decorated with murals and other artwork by Italian POWs from nearby Camp Hereford.

The POWs were paid a minimum wage consistent with civilian day laborers if they did work, at a rate of $30 per month for enlisted or $24 a month for officers who weren't allowed to work. Those men who did work were paid $0.80-1.20 per day depending on if working for local farmers or private companies. This was paid to them in coupons they could use at the Canteen, although ISU members could receive a third of their pay in cash to use in town. ISU members also received pay that was slightly higher, sometimes $1.50 per day to match the pay of American soldiers. That rate of pay was based on their rank in the ISU, not their Italian Army rank. An office of the Italian Army which made sure all the former POWs received their due pay was opened at the end of the war and continued until very recently. I worked in their offices in 2004 and was able to obtain records of transfers from camp to camp and the health record for a POW (with authorization from his son).

Geneva Convention required that officers be separated. They were sometimes in a compound next to the enlisted men and had otherwise the same types of facilities.

Above left: Murals painted by Italian POWs at St. Mary's Catholic Church at Umbarger (TX). [*Courtesy of John Saffell*]

Above right: A Papal Delegate visited the Italian POWs at Camp Weingarten (MO). [*Courtesy of Gary Reeves collection of POW artifacts*]

Above: Clearly, this isn't the first time the folks in town have seen POWs going past, the boy on a bicycle isn't even looking at them and the teenage girls are interested spectators. [*Courtesy of Gary Reeves collection of POW artifacts*]

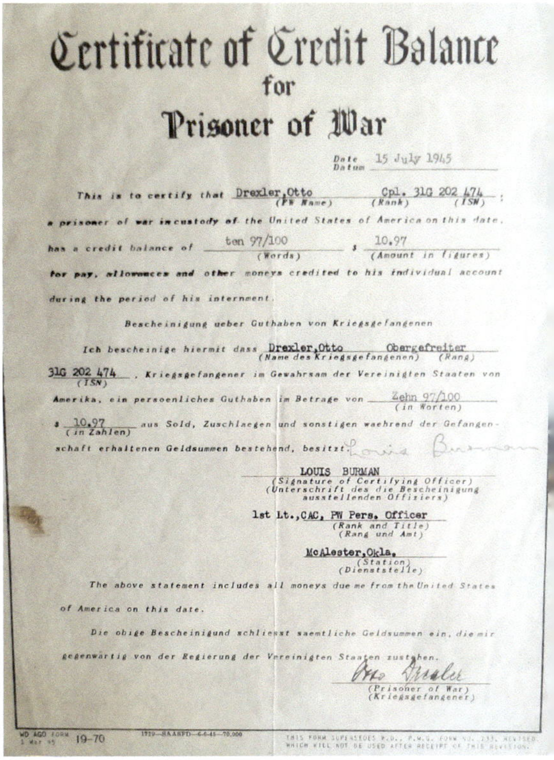

Certificate of Credit Balance
for
Prisoner of War

Date / Datum 15 July 1945

This is to certify that Drexler,Otto (PW Name) Cpl. (Rank) 31G 202 474 (ISN); a prisoner of war in custody of the United States of America on this date, has a credit balance of ten 97/100 (Words) $ 10.97 (Amount in figures) for pay, allowances and other moneys credited to his individual account during the period of his internment.

Bescheinigung ueber Guthaben von Kriegsgefangenen

Ich bescheinige hiermit dass Drexler,Otto (Name des Kriegsgefangenen) Obergefreiter (Rang) 31G 202 474 (ISN), Kriegsgefangener im Gewahrsam der Vereinigten Staaten von Amerika, ein persoenliches Guthaben im Betrage von Zehn 97/100 (in Worten) $ 10.97 (in Zahlen) aus Sold, Zuschlaegen und sonstigen waehrend der Gefangenschaft erhaltenen Geldsummen bestehend, besitzt.

LOUIS BURMAN
(Signature of Certifying Officer)
(Unterschrift des die Bescheinigung ausstellenden Offiziers)

1st Lt.,CAC, PW Pers. Officer
(Rank and Title)
(Rang und Amt)

McAlester,Okla.
(Station)
(Dienststelle)

The above statement includes all moneys due me from the United States of America on this date.

Die obige Bescheinigund schliesst saemtliche Geldsummen ein, die mir gegenwärtig von der Regierung der Vereinigten Staaten zustehen.

(Prisoner of War)
(Kriegsgefangener)

WD AGO FORM 19-70 1 Mar 45

THIS FORM SUPERSEDES W.D., P.M.G. FORM NO. 133, REVISED WHICH WILL NOT BE USED AFTER RECEIPT OF THIS REVISION.

Right: This form from Camp McAlester (OK) shows the accounting made by the US Army when the POWs were processed to return home. [*Courtesy of Gary Reeves collection of POW artifacts*]

Italian Service Units

The fall of Mussolini and resultant change in that government's position in the war from Axis to Allied required some changes regarding Italian POWs. It was quickly determined that releasing them would not be the best solution. The original idea of Italian POWs being organized into units to provide labor similar to the Civilian Conservation Corps (CCC) was first proposed by the US Secretary of War in October 1943. This would require separation of Fascist Italian POWs from those willing to work for the war effort as co-belligerents. They would be:

> attached to and placed under the command of the US Army ... Therefore, the plan included these features: (1) Italian prisoners would be organized into numbered Italian service companies consisting of 5 officers and 177 enlisted men ... (4) An Italian service unit headquarters would be established under ASF and would be commanded by an American officer...The new plan provided for Italian Service Units (ISUs) to be organized from volunteer Italian PW officers, non-commissioned officers, and enlisted men under approved tables of organization and equipment, less weapons. Initially, two US Army officers and 10 enlisted men were to be attached to each unit for supervision; but these were to be reduced, consistent with efficiency and security, to a minimum of one officer and five enlisted men.[1]

The ranking Italian General over the new ISU on 26 January 1944, Claudio Trezzani, states:

> The units should be commanded by Italian officers, in this proportion; one first or second lieutenant for 30 to 35 enlisted men (platoon), one captain for 4 platoons (company), one senior officer for 3 companies (battalion), one colonel for 3 battalions (regiment).[2]

That letter is followed in the Italian Army file at Stato Maggiore Esercito in Rome by an apparent American response with no name or date attached stating:

> It is contemplated organizing Italian Service Units according to American tables of organization with Italian military personnel in all authorized positions, American officers and enlisted men in the smallest possible numbers will be attached as custodians, for liaison, to issue operational directives, sign payrolls and charges, and have general responsibility for the units to higher American authority.[3]

Above: Italian Service Units at Utah ASF Depot. [*Courtesy of Special Collections Department, Stewart Library, Weber State University*]

Below: Italian Service Unit English Class at Camp Warren (WY). [*Courtesy of Gary Reeves collection of POW artifacts*]

Italian Generals Frattini and De Simone were moved to ISU headquarters at Fort Wadsworth from Camp Monticello.

The ISU program was under the command of Brig. General J. M. Eager, from the PMGO. The ASF retained the responsibilities of plans, policies and procedures as well as the designation and strength of units and training programs and doctrines. Each unit had American personnel of one officer and five enlisted men at a minimum. Service commands were responsible for all other ISU functions and activities. Interviews with former translators assigned to those units confirmed that one American NCO was a translator for the unit.

The ISU had increased responsibilities resulting in increased privileges for the sixty-five percent of Italian POWs who signed up to serve in Italian Service Units. The new units were activated progressively with 600 POWs organized in the first week of March 1944, 1,000 for the first two weeks of April, 3,000 the third week in April, and 4,000 each succeeding week until completed. While a letter was sent to the camps from Badoglio in Rome, it was vague and general and the Italian King never spoke or wrote on the subject. This left many men in confusion as to the best course of action. Their families were in German occupied Italy and many feared repercussions for such a visible support of their former enemy. The screening from ISU to POW and reverse was continuous to ensure that only the most cooperative POWs were allowed the privileges of the ISU.

Those men who signed the agreement to join the ISU were given new positions and units and now lived in separate compounds than the POWs who didn't sign the agreement.

Those POWs who didn't join the ISU were classified as Fascist. Instruction in English was stressed in these new units, while the same housing and wages applied, with the addition of ten cents a day for a gratuitous allowance, sometimes more depending on the work and on their ranks in the new units. Two-thirds of the wage was paid in coupons and one-third in cash. Rules against fraternization between members of ISU and American military did not apply. ISU Service Clubs were created to give them greater access to reading materials and a quiet place to relax since they did not have access to the US Army clubs. Dances and other special events were organized through the ISU Service Clubs.

Training programs for ISU was the same as for American personnel on similar jobs, with less tactics and weapons training.

Work restrictions imposed by Geneva Convention were lifted with the consent of the Badoglio government of Italy, except for combat, work at ports of embarkation within the continental US, and work with explosives. Their efforts released US personnel for overseas duties and helped to bring about the successful conclusion of the war.

ISU units began to ship to European Theater to assist with support and supply from Africa and into Italy as part of the Liberation of Italy in the following theaters of operation: North Africa, Eastern European, Mediterranean. Apparently, some of these units were moved overseas at the discretion of the ISU command and the PMGO was not informed.

Mail restrictions were reduced to the same standards as American personnel for domestic correspondence. Regulations were the same as POWs for international mail. The new ISU uniforms

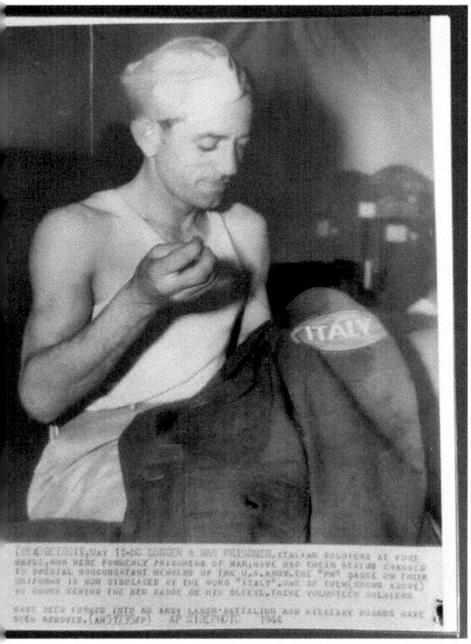

Above left: Sewing on his new ISU patch at Fort Wayne (MI). [*Courtesy of Gary Reeves collection of POW artifacts*]

Above right: Italian Service Club at Utah ASF Depot. [*Courtesy of Special Collections Department, Stewart Library, Weber State University*]

were the same khaki as US uniforms, with a patch (Italy) on the left shoulder. At least one man was court-martialed for removing the Italian patch on a night out on the town, leading to accusations of being AWOL. However, he was simply reprimanded instead of sent to a POW camp.

The POWs and their employers and guards weren't supposed to fraternize but, of course, they did. While some of the initial contact was antagonistic, many friendships and romances resulted.

ISU men were permitted weekend passes when signed out by a sponsor. Many Italian communities utilized these privileges to give some of the ISU men a family gathering, social activity, or dance. Some of the dances at the ISU Service Club included invitations to young women in the community.

Additionally, ISU members were given day passes into town for movies, dances, and just sightseeing. In Ogden, buses were used to transport ISU men from their barracks to St. Joseph's Catholic Church in downtown Ogden for dances. Of course, the greatest attraction was meeting and dancing with American girls.

Some of these meetings resulted in marriages. The POWs couldn't marry, but once engaged and returned (by June 1946), the troop transports bringing GIs home were taking these women with their escorts to Italy with the proper paperwork to marry so they could return to the US with their new husbands. Several of these couples settled in the Inland Empire of Northern California. Six of these men's experiences are described in detail in Susan Ann Meier's master's thesis.

Some of these meetings had unhappy endings. The local culture was against marrying a man of a different ethnic or religious background, plus some families feared that their girls would follow the men to Italy and never return. So those romances were discouraged, even after they created children. Some of those children were adopted out, while some stayed with their mothers who married other men here in the US after the war. Some of those children are sought their Italian families all their lives. Fortunately, we have assisted with some happy reunions.

Public opinion varied as shown in a variety of newspapers from those years. There were some escapes, usually associated with meeting a girl outside the camp for reasons that had nothing to do with national security.

The Italian POWs held a unique position as both POWs and allies that created different experiences for them than for their German counterparts. In Northern California and other ISU locations, these differences meant more opportunities to not only work with the residents, but also to socialize with them. The resulting friendships (and some marriages) show the very positive results of their experiences under very difficult circumstances.

1. Lewis, George G., and Mewha, John, *History of Prisoner of War Utilization by the United States Army, 1776-1945*, pamphlet 20-213 (US Department of the Army, Washington DC: Government Printing Office, 1955)
2. Trezzani, Claudio, "Letter from Monticello PW Camp, AR," 26 January 1944. Stato Maggiore Esercito, #2256A, Roma.
3. NARA RG 389, Entry 467, Box 1529

Death in the Camps

A total of 1,074 burials, including 880 Germans (includes three Russians, four Austrians, one Yugoslavian, one Czech and one Turk), 172 Italians, twenty-three Japanese (includes one Korean) out of 1,076 POWs who died while held in the US during World War II.

Many of the larger camps had their own cemeteries. After the war, the cemeteries from those camps which had been closed and some other locations, were moved to national cemeteries to provide the perpetual care demanded by the Geneva Convention.

While most of the headstones were standard issue for US military, there are some exceptions. At Fort Douglas, Eilert's stone was put up by the POWs with the permission of the camp commander and paid for by the POWs.

The funeral services were often attended by Americans as well as POWs, sometimes also either a POW choir, band, or both, and a symbolic series of shots fired by a military guard.

Rumors insist that most of the POWs who died here were shipped home. The truth is that the US government was willing to ship them if the family bore the cost. Of course, most of the families were simply unable to bear that burden at the end of a war they lost. Only one Italian, Renato Facchini, was returned to Italy before February 1947, while Francesco Erriquez was returned to Italy in 2011. Apparently, none of the Germans were returned since the names in the original reports match the current cemetery records.

Some of the deaths were accidents in the course of work or recreation. Others were later deemed murders by Nazi extremists. Some were suicides, particularly at the end of the war.

Above: This funeral was held at Camp Monticello, AR. [*Photo courtesy of Robert Todaro*]

Below left: The military honor guard with rifles for a military salute at a funeral at Camp Swift (TX). [*Courtesy of Gary Reeves collection of POW artifacts*]

Below right: Death cards were printed by the family back home in Germany and Italy. This one is for a man who died at Glendon (MN), a temporary camp under Camp Algona (IA). Someone thoughtfully attached a photo of his headstone located at Fort Riley (KS). [*Courtesy of Gary Reeves collection of POW artifacts*]

Returning Home (1945-46)

The end of the war was cause for celebration for the POWs who could now look forward to returning home. Their newsletters often contained cartoons expressing these feelings.
Certain camps were designated as separation centers (like Haan, CA) and the POWs were moved through them, then on to ports of embarkation on both coasts for the trip home. The first returned were the Italian officers as co-belligerents. The next group was the ISU members, then the rest.

Geneva Convention of 1929 required that POWs be returned home at the end of a war. However, the large numbers provided some logistical problems. Generally, troop ships bringing US troops home turned around full of POWs. However, treaties with all countries provided that some of the POWs (not ISU) were returned to France, the USSR, and Great Britain to assist with reconstruction efforts. Some of the men in Great Britain and France worked there as long as four years before returning home. The USSR finally released the surviving German prisoners ten years later, after releasing Italian prisoners in 1947.

Warnings were made regarding German POWs scheduled to be returned to their families and homes in the USSR. It was only after the first group was killed on the dock by the crew of the Soviet vessel which met them that other arrangements were made for those men.

Some POWs claimed status as US citizens and requested permission to stay but were returned to avoid the legal complications.

Some locations requested that their POWs stay long enough to complete the fall harvest and that was permitted when it could be arranged. The last POWs were repatriated (out of the US) by 30 June 1946 except 141 Germans, twenty Italians, and one Japanese serving sentences in US Penal Institutions. Not repatriated were two Germans who revealed themselves many years later, perhaps more since none are shown as missing on PMGO reports.

A large number of ports were utilized as departure points for the returning POWs. They included:

Los Angeles, CA
Charleston, SC
New Orleans, LA
Hampton Roads, VA
New York, NY
Boston, MA
San Francisco, CA
Seattle, WA
Halifax, Nova Scotia

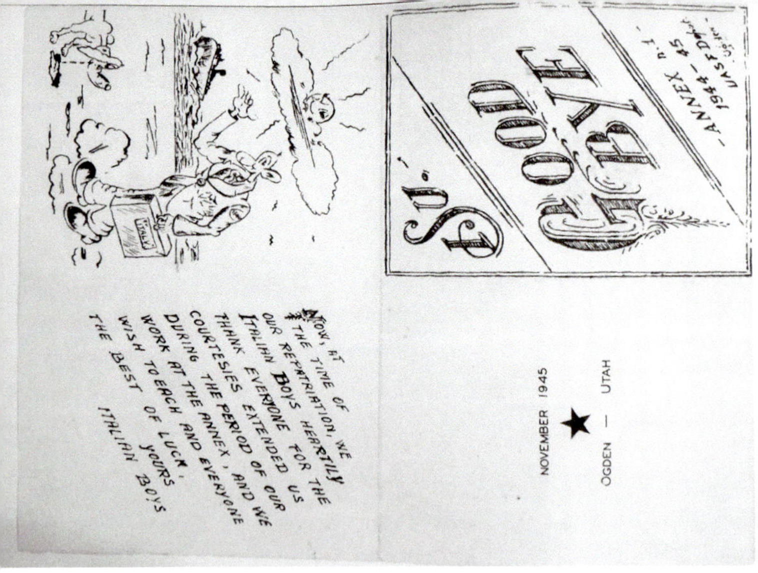

This goodbye note from the Italian Boys at Utah ASF Depot was saved by Mario Saggese, one of those boys, and used here courtesy of his daughter, living in the United States.

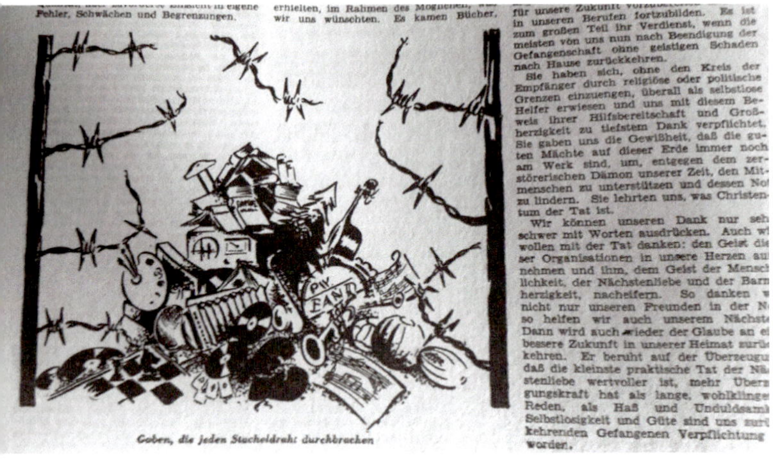

Fehler, Schwächen und Begrenzungen.

erhielten, im Rahmen des Möglichen, was wir uns wünschten. Es kamen Bücher,

für unsere Zukunft ...
in unseren Berufen fortzubilden. Es ist
zum großen Teil ihr Verdienst, wenn die
meisten von uns nun nach Beendigung der
Gefangenschaft ohne geistigen Schaden
nach Hause zurückkehren.
Sie haben sich, ohne den Kreis der
Empfänger durch religiöse oder politische
Grenzen einzuengen, überall als selbstlose
Helfer erwiesen und uns mit diesem Be-
weis ihrer Hilfsbereitschaft und Groß-
herzigkeit zu tiefstem Dank verpflichtet.
Sie gaben uns die Gewißheit, daß die gu-
ten Mächte auf dieser Erde immer noch
am Werk sind, um, entgegen dem zer-
störerischen Dämon unserer Zeit, den Mit-
menschen zu unterstützen und dessen Not
zu lindern. Sie lehrten uns, was Christen-
tum der Tat ist.
Wir können unseren Dank nur seh
schwer mit Worten ausdrücken. Auch wi
wollen mit der Tat danken: den Geist die
ser Organisationen in unsere Herzen au
nehmen und ihm, dem Geist der Mensch
lichkeit, der Nächstenliebe und der Barm
herzigkeit, nacheifern. So danken w
nicht nur unseren Freunden in der N
so helfen wir auch unserem Nächste
Dann wird auch wieder der Glaube an ei
bessere Zukunft in unserer Heimat zurüc
kehren. Er beruht auf der Überzeugu
daß die kleinste praktische Tat der Nä
stenliebe wertvoller ist, mehr Überz
gungskraft hat als lange, wohlklinge
Reden, als Haß und Unduldsamk
Selbstlosigkeit und Güte sind uns zurü
kehrenden Gefangenen Verpflichtung
worden.

Gaben, die jeden Stacheldraht durchbrachen

The broken barbed wire and discarded items of entertainment show that while their time as prisoners is ended, so is their leisure time since they now need to rebuild their homes and families. [*Courtesy of Gary Reeves collection of POW artifacts*]

This cartoon showing the camp for sale is much more lighthearted. [*Courtesy of Gary Reeves collection of POW artifacts*]

Those same troop vessels were used to transport American fiancés of POWs to Naples and Genoa. These American war brides often spent a few months in Italy to complete the red tape required for a marriage there and assisting their new families in rebuilding. They then brought their husbands home to America. These stories were shared by Pat and Maria Pisani and by Beth Giordana, war brides and American girls who made the trip to Italy to marry their former POW husbands.

Part of the logistics meant that after the US troops returned home, their European war brides and families were shipped home on the same troop ships, slightly modified to accommodate families with small children. Be sure to see the Cary Grant movie, *I Was a Male War Bride*, more funny than factual, but it is based on the real transport of war brides from Europe to America.

Other former POWs made the move to live in the US from ten to twenty years later. They settled in areas where they had worked as POWs, apparently in nearly every location in the country. Only local newspapers have these stories, so it's hard to get statistics. I recently found an article, "Returning to America: German Prisoners of War and the American Experience" by Barbara Schmitter Heisler, details in the bibliography.

The trip to marry in Italy was made by a young woman from Louisville, KY who had met her husband when he was a prisoner at Camp Atterbury, Indiana. They'd met at a dance sponsored by the local Italian-American community for the Italian POWs. I met this lovely woman at a POW reunion at Camp Atterbury in 2010 along with her children. They were regular attendees at this annual event and had wonderful stories to share. They also have a display at the Camp Atterbury Museum, across the road from the main gate to Camp Atterbury, now a reserve military training facility.

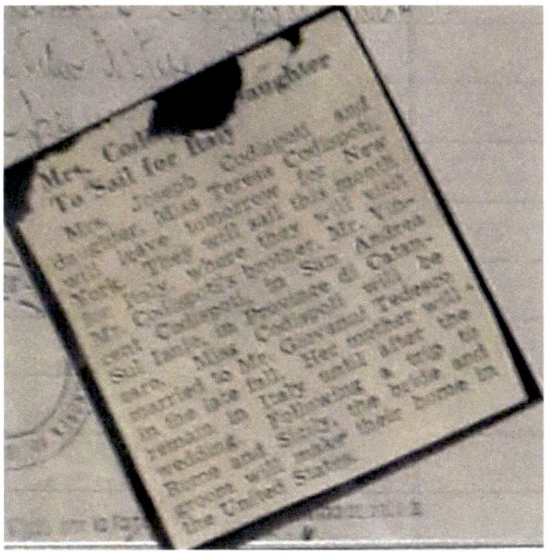

Above left: A portion of the museum display of the Codispoti family, a former Italian POW who settled in the area of Camp Atterbury (IN). [*Photo by author*]

Above right: This book of art was apparently created during his POW years and published later. [*Courtesy of Gary Reeves collection of POW artifacts*]

After the War

Some of the camps were determined to be surplus, so the property was auctioned off and the land was sold or transferred to another federal or state agency. This was a thorough process, leaving behind very little in the way of buildings to mark the former camps today.

Some of the locations had their designations changed from camp to fort, some were originally forts, but were called camps along with the rest in the PMGO records.

The POW personnel records were returned to other nations in whose military they served in 1955. The German records are now available at:

Deutsche Dienstelle (WASt)
Postfach 51 06 57
D-13400 Berlin
Germany

The Italian records are now available at:

Ministero della Difesa
via Mattia Battistini, 113, 7 Piano
00167 Roma
Italy

The Japanese records are now available at:

Military History Department National Institute for Defense Studies
2-2-1 Nakameguro, Meguro-ku
Tokyo, 153-8648
Japan

The former POWs held in the US mostly held good memories of their time here. Some returned to become US citizens, like Ernst Bulkat who lived in Orem, UT. Information on them can usually be found in local papers in the 1970s and 1980s when local news groups interviewed them in a resurgence of interest in the history of the area during WWII.

Some former POWs returned as tourists to show their families where they'd spent part of the war. Some groups held reunions of groups of POWs who had been at a particular location to facilitate their return there with some ceremony and lots of memories.

Some diaries and recollections have been published by former POWs. See Erichsen, Heino R. *The Reluctant Warrior: Former German POW Finds Peace in Texas* for the story of a man who later became a US citizen. The grandson of one of the Italian Generals, Maurizio Parri, published his grandfather's war time diaries in *Il Giuramento; Generale a El Alamein, prigioniero in America (1942-1945).*

Some former POWs have been gracious about allowing interviews at reunions, such as Adriano Angerilli, Enzio Luciolli, Giuseppe Margotilli, Fernando Togni (pictured above). Some of the former, guards, prisoners and their families have become available for interviews using email, like Ernst Bulkat, Mario Iannantuoni and August Orsini. On other occasions I have been able to interview the children or grandchildren of a former POW in Italy or the US.

In 2009, one of the last reunions of former POWs visited the chapel built by POWs at Camp Hereford, TX. This is indicative of a growing awareness that these memories and relationships must be preserved through reunions, books, lectures and movies.

Some local magazines and newspapers have done stories on the camps and published interviews with former POWs returning to visit, or who had moved back to the area where they'd been imprisoned. Some of these have been preserved by the newspaper, some by local historians, colleges, and historical societies.

A documentary video, *Prisoners in Paradise*, DVD, directed by Camilla Calamandrei, tells some of the stories of former Italian POWs, a couple from Utah.

Some local TV stations did interviews with surviving former POWs living in their communities in the 1970s and 1980s, like KUED and KSL in Salt Lake City, UT. Some local colleges (Special Collections, Stewart Library, Weber State University), created video archives containing interviews of former POWs and their families and former guards and other employees who had interaction with POWs.

Some former POWs, guards, and their families donated their diaries and photos to local historical societies, like Drew County Historical Museum, Monticello, Arkansas. Some donated to the National Archives (NARA) in College Park, Maryland. Some donated to the Stato Maggiore Esercito in Rome, Italy. I expect more will be found in local colleges and libraries in America, Italy, and Germany.

Former guards, like Thomas Todaro and Peter A. Pulia, Sr. also shared their memories in interviews and photos. Some, like Ralph Storm, wrote books about their experiences with POWs.

Even today, I receive emails from the children and grandchildren of former POWs to learn more about the experiences of being a POW in the US and the hope of locating records regarding their work, health, and transfers. Most of these former POWs do not or did not talk about their experiences. Mario Turrini only told his children that Hawaii was nice, no comment on his service in Greece, Tunisia, or his experiences at the other camps where he was held in the US.

This photo was taken at the 2009 reunion at Camp Hereford (TX). The US Army is on the left, the former POWs center, and the Italian Air Force on the right. [*Photo by John Saffell of these men in front of the Chapel built by Italian POWs*]

A belt buckle and lariat created for a reunion at Camp Atlanta (NE). [*Courtesy of Gary Reeves collection of POW artifacts*]

Former POW's Remember

Howard Noel, Channel 5 News   Joe Giordana   Gene Maconi

Gene Maconi and Joe Giordana took time this week to recount stories of the Italian POW camp which later became a service organization located here during World War II. Channel 5 News stopped by to film the occasion as sites of the old facilities were remembered. Mr. Maconi is the operator of a tile company in Ogden and Mr. Giordana is a Depot employee assigned to the Directorate of Installation Services. Both Mr. Maconi and Mr. Giordana went back to Italy after the war but returned to Ogden to make their homes. Asked why they came back both had the same answer – "To marry a local girl."

Right: Photo of TV interview of Joe Giordana and Gene Miconi about their POW years in Utah ASF Depot. [*Courtesy of Special Collections Department, Stewart Library, Weber State University*]

Below: Wilson Longo (named for Woodrow Wilson) was born and died in Bellosguardo, Italy. He was a prisoner at Utah ASF Depot. His cousin, Barbara, provided this photo and information.

Some of these letters come from Italy, but some also come from England, Australia, and the United States where these men took their families after the war.

These memories can assist us in planning for the future, promoting the preservation of photos and artifacts from the POW camps. Preservation of these memories can also be achieved by conducting interviews of surviving former POWs and their guards, and members of the community.

We can use these memories and memorabilia to educate public about the policies and experiences of WWII and to promote the good treatment of future POWs.

Mary Ravarino with photos and letters from the Italian POWs from Utah ASF Depot who worked on her family's farm in Salt Lake City area. [*Photo courtesy of Italian Center of the West (UtahCulturalNews.com)*]

POW Camps by Location

There were 1,204 prisoner of par camps, Italian Service Unit Camps, and Prisoner of War Hospitals in the US.

The camp lists at NARA shows several APO addresses in place of camp names. Judging by the dates, these were located in the Philippines, Hawaii, and New Caledonia.

In Northern California, there were over 10,500 German, over 3,000 Italian, and over 3,500 Japanese POWS in fifty-nine POW camps and hospitals as follows:

Angel Island, Tiburon, Marin County, CA (Prisoner of War Processing) (base camp), part of San Francisco Port of Embarkation, includes Fort McDowell, a California State Park since 1958. The camp opened in August 1943. At maximum, it held sixty-three German POWs in August 1943 and 769 Japanese POWs in June 1945.

Arbuckle, Colusa County, CA (branch camp under Beale). The camp opened in May 1945. The camp was originally part of the Emergency Rubber Project of the Department of Agriculture, trying to extract rubber from the Guayule shrub. That project closed in September 1944 and transferred the land to the Army in March 1945. At maximum, it held 503 German POWs in September 1945. The work was agricultural in the nearby almond groves. In 1946 the camp returned to the Rubber project and auctioned off in 1948.

Ashview, Madera County, CA (branch camp under Ord) (see Chowchilla). The work was agricultural. At maximum, the camp held 250 German POWs in January 1945.

Bacon Island, San Joaquin County, CA (branch camp under Stockton). The camp opened in June 1945. At maximum, the camp held 251 German POWs in June 1945. The work was agricultural.

Beale (Camp Edward F.), Yuba County, CA (base camp), now Beale Air Force Base, an active military installation. It was named for a man who graduated from the US Naval Academy, served in the California State Militia, led the experiment to replace army mules with camels during the Civil War, and was one of California's largest landowners. The base maintains and preserves thirty-eight Native American sites, forty-five homestead sites, and forty-one World War II sites on it's 23,000 acres. The POW camp opened in May 1944. It had been requested by Marysville City. In 1942 it was a training post for the 13th Armored Division as well as training facilities for the 81st and 96th Infantry Divisions. A hospital was also built here. At maximum, the camp held 4,102 German POWs in September 1945. The work was military, agricultural, and more. Camp Beale cemetery contained three German and three Italian WWII POW burials later transferred to Golden Gate National Cemetery.

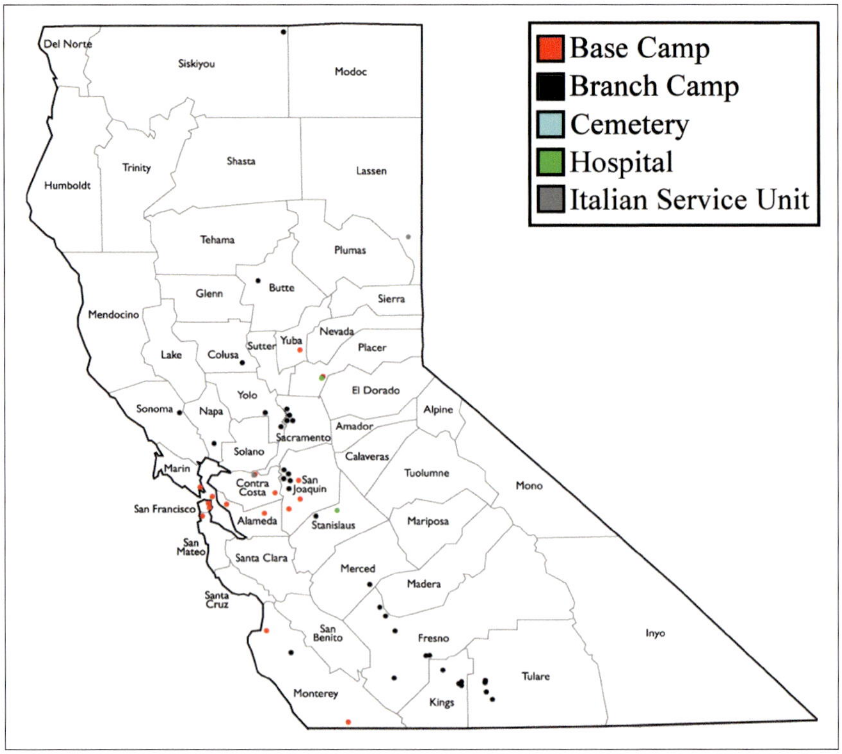
Base Camp
Branch Camp
Cemetery
Hospital
Italian Service Unit
Del Norte
Siskiyou
Modoc
Humboldt
Trinity
Shasta
Lassen
Tehama
Plumas
Glenn
Butte
Sierra
Mendocino
Nevada
Sutter
Yuba
Placer
Lake
Colusa
Yolo
El Dorado
Sonoma
Napa
Alpine
Amador
Sacramento
Solano
Calaveras
Marin
Tuolumne
Contra Costa
San Joaquin
Mono
San Francisco
Alameda
Stanislaus
Mariposa
San Mateo
Santa Clara
Merced
Madera
Santa Cruz
San Benito
Fresno
Inyo
Tulare
Monterey
Kings

WATER TANKS
STAFF HOUSING
MAIN WATER SUPPLY (CISTERN)
COVERED EXERCISE YARD
HOSPITAL
BARRACKS
DINING ROOM
ADMINISTRATION BUILDING
PIER TO CHINA COVE

Opposite above: Map showing POW camps and hospitals in Northern California. [*Courtesy of John Saffell*]

Opposite below: Angel Island. [*Courtesy of Carol A. Jensen, historian at Byron Hot Springs*]

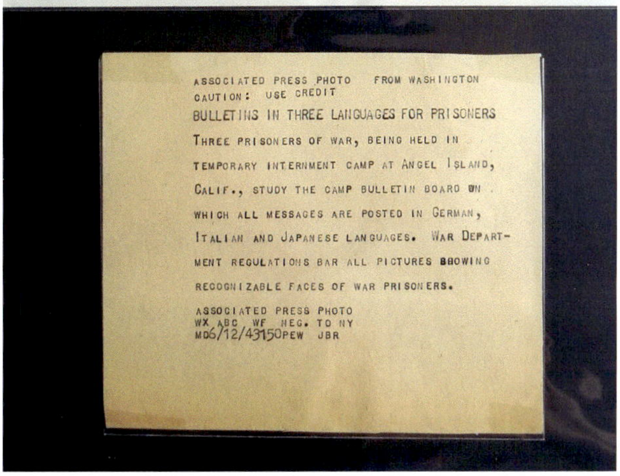

ASSOCIATED PRESS PHOTO FROM WASHINGTON
CAUTION: USE CREDIT
BULLETINS IN THREE LANGUAGES FOR PRISONERS
THREE PRISONERS OF WAR, BEING HELD IN TEMPORARY INTERNMENT CAMP AT ANGEL ISLAND, CALIF., STUDY THE CAMP BULLETIN BOARD ON WHICH ALL MESSAGES ARE POSTED IN GERMAN, ITALIAN AND JAPANESE LANGUAGES. WAR DEPARTMENT REGULATIONS BAR ALL PICTURES SHOWING RECOGNIZABLE FACES OF WAR PRISONERS.
ASSOCIATED PRESS PHOTO
WX ABC WF NEG. TO NY
MD6/12/43150PEW JBR

Right: Angel Island Announcements in three languages. [*Courtesy of Carol A. Jensen, historian at Byron Hot Springs*]

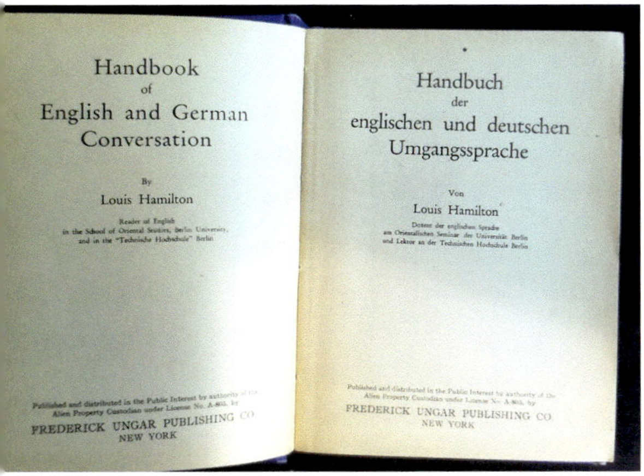

From Camp Beale, German English Conversation book. [*Courtesy of Gary Reeves collection of POW artifacts*]

Benicia Arsenal, Pittsburg, Contra Costa County, CA (ISU). The camp opened in September 1945. This located first housed Army infantry in 1849 and became the first Ordnance Supply Depot in the West in 1851. The Army's only Camel Corps was stabled here from 1855 until disbanded in 1863. However, the Camel Barns are now the Benicia Historical Museum. The POW camp opened in September 1945. The Benicia Arsenal Post Cemetery, is now in the care of the National Park Service. This cemetery contains one Italian and eight German WWII POW burials.

Boswell Ranch, near Corcoran, Kings County, CA (branch camp under Cooke, sometimes under Lamont). The camp opened in August 1945. At maximum, the camp held 254 German POWs in August and then 717 Japanese POWs from Camp McCoy in Wisconsin and Camp Clarinda in Iowa in December 1945. The work was agricultural and other. The camp closed in January 1946.

Bouldin Island, San Joaquin County, CA (branch camp under Stockton). This camp opened in May 1945. At maximum, it held 261 German POW in October 1945, doing agricultural work.

Byron Hot Springs, Contra Costa County, CA (restricted listing, interrogation center). This camp was originally a health spa. It was used for interrogation by the US Army and sometimes called Camp Tracy, sometimes called PO Box 651. This is because such centers were a violation of the Geneva Conventions, so the location was disguised as a processing center. The camp was divided into two sections, one German and one Japanese. From December 1942 to July 1945, over 3,500 Japanese POWs were interrogated at this location. 645 German POWs were interrogated here in 1944, but the maximum at any one time was only fifty-one. The camp was closed in September 1945 and again became the resort called Byron Hot Springs.

Benicia Camel Barns. [*Photo by author*]

Above left: Byron Hot Springs Front Entrance. [*Courtesy of Carol A. Jensen, historian at Byron Hot Springs*]

Above right: Byron Hot Springs Fenced. [*Courtesy of Carol A. Jensen, historian at Byron Hot Springs*]

Above left: Byron Hot Springs Barred Windows. [*Courtesy of Carol A. Jensen, historian at Byron Hot Springs*]

Above right: Byron Hot Springs Mud Baths. [*Courtesy of Carol A. Jensen, historian at Byron Hot Springs*]

Chico (Camp), Butte County, CA (branch camp under Beale). This camp opened in September 1945. At maximum, it held 475 German POWs in September 1945.

Chowchilla, Madera County, CA (branch camp under Ord, see Ashview). This camp opened in January 1944. The maximum population was 340 German POWs in November 1945.

Clarksburg, Yolo County, CA (branch camp under Stockton). This camp opened in May 1945. At maximum population was 460 German POWs during agricultural work in April 1946.

Coalinga, Fresno County, CA (branch camp under Ord). The camp opened in November 1945. At maximum, the population was 250 German POWs in November 1945.

Corcoran, Kings County, CA (branch camp under Cooke, sometimes Stockton) (see Lakeland). This camp opened in December 1944. At maximum, the population was 500 German POWs in December 1944. They picked cotton on the Gilkey and Boswell ranches.

Corcoran No. 2, Kings County, CA (branch camp under Cooke). This camp opened in May of 1946. The maximum population was 410 German POWs.

Dairyland, Madera County, CA (branch camp under Ord. The camp opened in January 1944. At maximum, the population was 367 German POWs in November 1945, doing agricultural work.

Davis, Yolo County, CA (branch camp under Beale). The camp opened in August 1945. At maximum, it held 250 German POWs in August 1945.

DeWitt (Calvin) General Hospital, Auburn, Placer County, CA (base camp), later a state hospital until 1972, now DeWitt Government Center. The hospital opened in February 1944, the POW camp opened in June 1944. At maximum it held one Japanese patient in July 1944, 200 German POW workers in July 1945. The work was classified as military, although POW workers at a hospital were usually doing landscaping and housekeeping. It was declared surplus in December 1945 and in March 1947 it was quitclaimed to the State of California.

Dos Palos, Merced County, CA (branch camp under Ord). The camp opened in October 1945. It was located at an old Civilian Conservation Corps Camp with guard towers and security fences added. The maximum population was 200 German POWs in October 1945.

Firebaugh, Fresno County, CA (branch camp under Ord). The camp opened in May 1945. The maximum population was 746 German POWs in November 1945, doing agricultural work.

Five Points No. 1, Fresno County, CA (branch camp under Ord). The camp opened in January 1944. At maximum, it held 501 German POWs in November 1945 doing agricultural work.

Five Points No. 2, Fresno County, CA (branch camp under Ord). The camp opened in November 1945. At maximum, it held 401 German POWs in November 1945.

Flint (Camp), Auburn, Placer County, CA (former Civilian Conversation Corps camp) (branch camp under DeWitt (Calvin) General Hospital), now part of the fairgrounds. The men worked on public works projects in the Auburn area and lived here in wood and canvas hutments. In November 1940, the area was quitclaimed by the City of Auburn, but closed in July 1941 due to lack of funding. In December 1941, the 32nd Infantry used this location as their base of operations for providing defense of the railroad. Different Army organizations used this location until August 1944 when it came under the control of DeWitt General Hospital. In

June 1945, German POWs were transferred here from Florence, AZ to work at DeWitt General Hospital. The prisoners were last here in February 1946. Local stories relate that most of the visitors to the POW camp belonged to the local Italian community, bringing cookies and cakes to the prisoners.

Hammond (William A.) General Hospital, Modesto, Stanislaus County, CA, now Yosemite Junior College and Stanislaus County Juvenile Justice Center. The hospital was built in 1942 by the Army to treat war wounded. The POW camp opened in March 1944. At maximum, it held 3 Italian POW patients in March 1944 and two German POW patients in September 1945. The hospital closed in December 1945 and was turned over to the state.

King Island, San Joaquin County, CA (branch camp under Stockton). The camp opened in May 1945. At maximum, it held 251 German POWs in May 1945 doing agricultural work.

Knight (Camp John Thornton), Oakland, Alameda County, part of San Francisco Port of Embarkation, now Oakland Army Base. The camp was named for John Thornton Knight, an Army General who worked as Quarter Master during World War I. This area was the administrative and cantonment area of what is now Oakland Army Base. It opened for POWs in September 1945. At maximum, the population was 824 German POWs in September 1945.

Kohler (Camp Fredrick L.), Sacramento, Sacramento County, CA (branch camp under Stockton). The camp opened in July 1945. At maximum, it held 1,051 German POWs in July 1945.

Lakeland, Kings County, CA (branch camp under Cooke) (see Corcoran). The camp opened in May 1945. The location was originally planned to house Mexican national expected to participate in the cotton harvest. When available Mexican nationals were used elsewhere, the von Glahn Lakeland Company requested POW labor. At maximum, it held 691 German POWs in March 1945, later it held 1296 Japanese POWs from Camp McCoy in Wisconsin and Camp Clarinda in Iowa in October 1945, doing agricultural work. They harvested cotton and fruit in the surrounding area. In January 1946, the Japanese POWs were moved in preparation to returning home and German POWs did the agricultural work for another few weeks. The camp closed in February 1946.

Lathrop Engineering Depot, Lathrop, San Joaquin County, CA (branch camp under Stockton, later a base camp). The camp opened in September 1945. At maximum, the population was 174 Italian Service Unit members in September 1945.

Lemoore, Kings County, CA (branch camp under Cooke), now Lemoore Naval Air Station. This location was an Army Air Field from December 1941. The POW camp opened in November 1945. At maximum, it held 2516 German POWs in March 1946. The camp closed in April 1946.

Letterman (Jonathan) General Hospital, San Francisco city and county, CA (base camp). The hospital was completed in March 1941. The POW camp opened in July 1944. At maximum, it held twelve Italian POW patients in June 1944, later twenty-three Japanese POW patients in December 1944, later six German POW patients in August 1945. In March 1945, 176 Italian POWs worked here doing work classified as military. Hospital records show that they furnished labor for the hospital. In December 1945, the Italian POWs were replaced by 150 German POWs who left for the New York Port of Embarkation in June 1946.

Italian POWs at Camp Knight. [*Courtesy of Gary Reeves collection of POW artifacts*]

Madera, Madera County, CA (branch camp under Ord). The camp opened in January 1945. At maximum, it held 250 German POWs in January 1945, doing agricultural work.

McClellan Field, Sacramento, Sacramento County, CA (branch camp under Stockton. The camp opened in April 1946. At maximum, it held 514 German POWs in May 1946.

McDowell (Fort), Angel Island, Marin County, CA (base camp, previously branch camp under San Francisco Port of Embarkation). This located began as Camp Reynolds (Major-General John) in 1863. The name was changed to that of the San Francisco General McDowell. In 1910 the Immigration Station was built there, and it was a recruit depot during World War I. It was then a discharge depot in 1922. From the start of the war, it served as a POW processing center before shipment to other camps in the interior. The first POW from Pearl Harbor was processed here. The POW camp opened (on PMGO reports) in September 1945. At maximum, it held 212 Italian Service Unit members in September 1945. The location was then a processing center for returning troops brought home from the Pacific Theaters and classified as surplus in August 1946.

Mendota, Fresno County, CA (branch camp under Ord). The camp opened in October 1945. At maximum, it held 500 German POWs in December 1945.

Napa, Napa County, CA (branch camp under Beale). The camp opened in September 1945. At maximum, it held 250 German POWs in September 1945.

Ord (Fort), Monterey County, CA (base camp), now used by the new California State University at Monterey, a research center for UC Santa Cruz, the Monterey Institute of International Studies, and the US Army. The fort was established in 1917 as a military training base for infantry troops. The POW camp opened in April 1944. At maximum, it held 2,414 German POWs and 302 Italian Service Unit members in September 1945 (separate compounds, same location). There was an unsuccessful attempt by 500 German POWs to escape through tunnels in August 1944. Fort Ord was a basic training center from 1947-1975.

Presidio of San Francisco, San Francisco County, CA (base camp) (see San Francisco Port of Embarkation). The POW camp opened in September 1945. At maximum, it held 433 Italian POWs in September 1945.

Rankin Field, Tulare County, CA (branch camp under Cooke). The camp opened in December 1945. This location was originally Rankin Aeronautical Academy as a private flying school under contract to the federal government to train pilots during WWII. They trained over 10,000 pilots. That contract was terminated in July 1945. Four months later, the San Joaquin Agricultural Labor Bureau contracted with the owners to use the location to house POWs to harvest cotton. At maximum, it held 737 German POWs in February 1946, closing that same month.

Rindge Tract, San Joaquin County, CA (branch camp under Stockton). The camp opened in June 1945. At maximum, it held 250 German POWs in June 1945 doing agricultural work.

Roberts (Camp Harold W.), San Miguel, Monterey County, CA (initially under Hill Field, UT, sometimes a base camp), now a National Guard facility. It's located along Hwy 101, a scenic drive along the old Mission Trail. While the site was originally surveyed by Army Engineers in 1902, it wasn't authorized until 1940. The original name was changed from Camp Nacimiento (for an

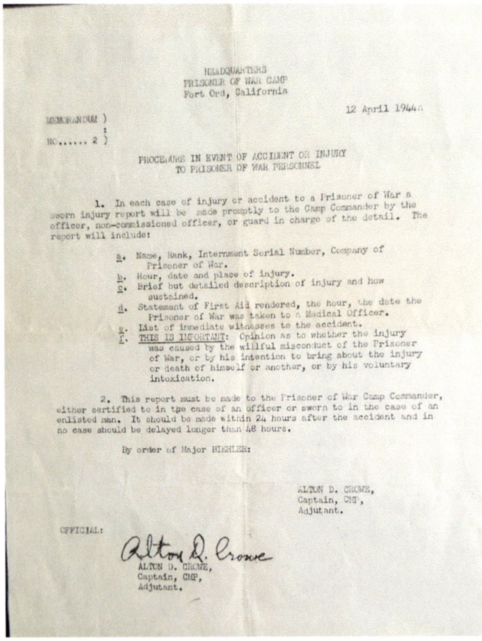

HEADQUARTERS
PRISONER OF WAR CAMP
Fort Ord, California

12 April 1944

MEMORANDUM)
:
NO...... 2)

PROCEDURE IN EVENT OF ACCIDENT OR INJURY
TO PRISONER OF WAR PERSONNEL

1. In each case of injury or accident to a Prisoner of War a sworn injury report will be made promptly to the Camp Commander by the officer, non-commissioned officer, or guard in charge of the detail. The report will include:

a. Name, Rank, Internment Serial Number, Company of Prisoner of War.
b. Hour, date and place of injury.
c. Brief but detailed description of injury and how sustained.
d. Statement of First Aid rendered, the hour, the date the Prisoner of War was taken to a Medical Officer.
e. List of immediate witnesses to the accident.
f. THIS IS IMPORTANT: Opinion as to whether the injury was caused by the willful misconduct of the Prisoner of War, or by his intention to bring about the injury or death of himself or another, or by his voluntary intoxication.

2. This report must be made to the Prisoner of War Camp Commander, either certified to in the case of an officer or sworn to in the case of an enlisted man. It should be made within 24 hours after the accident and in no case should be delayed longer than 48 hours.

By order of Major BIEHLER:

ALTON D. CROWE,
Captain, CMP,
Adjutant.

OFFICIAL:

Alton D. Crowe
ALTON D. CROWE,
Captain, CMP,
Adjutant.

Left: Fort Ord, POW Accident Reporting Memo. [*Courtesy of Gary Reeves collection of POW artifacts*]

Below: Rankin Field. [*Image located at www.wikipedia.org*]

original Spanish Land Grant) to Camp Roberts for a corporal, a WWI tank driver who lost his life in action in the Montrebeau Forest in France. It started as a training center with a hospital. The POW camp opened in September 1944. At maximum, it held 1,118 German POWs in July 1945, later it held 761 Italian POWs in November 1945, doing work classified as military. There were separate compounds for the German and Italian POWs who worked there.

Roberts Island, San Joaquin County, CA (branch camp under Stockton). The camp opened in October 1944. At maximum, it held 300 German POWs in October 1944 doing agricultural work.

Sacramento Signal Depot, Sacramento County, CA (branch camp under Stockton). The camp opened in October 1945. At maximum, it held 512 German POWs in February 1946, doing military work.

San Francisco Port of Embarkation, San Francisco, San Francisco County, CA (see Knight, Fort McDowell, Presidio of San Francisco, Stoneman). The POW camp opened November 1945. At maximum, it held 927 Italian POWs in November 1945.

San Joaquin, San Joaquin County, CA (branch camp under Ord). The camp opened in November 1945. At maximum, it held 500 German POWs in November 1945 doing agricultural and military work.

San Joaquin Fairgrounds, San Joaquin County, CA (branch camp under Stockton). Camp opened in October 1944. At maximum, it held 1517 German POWs in September 1945.

Sharp Park, San Mateo County, CA (Italian POW processing).

Shoemaker Naval Distribution Center, Livermore, Alameda County, CA (base camp), part of "Fleet City." The camp opened in August 1945. At maximum, it held 800 German POWs in September 1945.

Sierra Ordnance Depot, Herlong, Lassen County, CA (Italian Service Unit members).

Soledad, Monterey County, CA (branch camp under Ord). Originally part of the Emergency Rubber Project under the Department of Agriculture, it transferred to the War Department in 1944. The POW camp opened in October 1944. At maximum, it held 499 German POWs in October 1944 doing agricultural and other work. The camp closed in 1946.

Stockton (Camp) Ordnance Depot, Stockton, San Joaquin County, CA (base camp). The location was built as a supply depot in 1941. Also known as Quartermaster Motor Depot and as Stockton Motor Repair Depot. It became Stockton Ordnance Base in January 1943. The POW camp opened in May 1944. At maximum, it held 6873 German POWs in February 1946 and then three Italian POWs in May 1946. They did military and agricultural work.

Stoneman (Camp), Pittsburg, Contra Costa County, CA, part of San Francisco Port of Embarkation (base camp) (see San Francisco Port of Embarkation). The location was acquired by the War Department in 1942 for troop training. The POW camp opened in July 1945. At maximum, it held 418 Italian Service Unit members September 1945, then 2251 German POWs in February 1946.

Tachi Farms, Corcoran Kings County, CA (branch camp under Cooke). The camp opened in December 1945. It was located in the old Tulare Lake bed. At maximum, it held 250 German POWs in December 1945. They arrived here from the POW camp at Glasgow, MT. They harvested cotton. The camp closed in January 1946.

San Francisco Port of Embarkation. [*Courtesy of Carol A. Jensen, historian at Byron Hot Springs*]

Camp Stoneman Entrance. [*Courtesy of Carol A. Jensen, historian at Byron Hot Springs*]

Above left: Camp Stockton Concert Program, Stockton Concert. [*Courtesy of Gary Reeves collection of POW artifacts*]

Above right: Camp Stoneman Christmas Card. [*Courtesy of Tracy Historical Museum*]

Below: Camp Stoneman Garrison. [*Courtesy of Carol A. Jensen, historian at Byron Hot Springs*]

Tagus Ranch, Tulare County, CA (branch camp under Cooke). The camp opened in August 1944. The camp was ten miles north of Tulare on the west side of the railroad tracks off Hwy 99. The camp had been requested by the Tagus Ranch Company to work in the orchards and cotton fields. Prisoners from Camp Cooke helped construct the camp here and at other locations. There was a medical clinic here with a US Army doctor and two German Medical Corps prisoners. Those needing hospitalization were transported to Lemoor. The camp pets included dogs and cats as normal, but also doves. At maximum, the camp held 497 German POWs in December 1945, doing agricultural work. The camp closed in February 1946.

Tipton, Tulare County, CA (branch camp under Cooke). The camp opened in June 1945. It was located south of Tulare off Hwy 99. It had been used to house Mexican nationals doing agricultural work in the area. The Tulare Procurement Association requested POW labor and modified the camp for POW use. At maximum, it held 650 German POWs in December 1945, doing agricultural work. They harvested cotton and fruit in the area. The camp closed in February 1946.

Tracy Quartermaster Sub-Depot, Tracy, San Joaquin County, CA (branch camp under Stockton, sometimes a base camp). The camp opened in April 1945. At maximum, it held 757 German POWs in June 1945.

Tranquility, Fresno County, CA (branch camp under Ord). The camp opened in December 1945. At maximum, it held 510 German POWs in December 1945.

Treasure Island Naval Training and Distribution Center, San Francisco city and county, CA (base camp). Originally the island was built for the 1939-1940 Golden Gate International Exposition

Camp Tracy Christmas Card. [*Courtesy of Tracy Historical Museum*]

and a base for Pan American Airways. The Navy took over the island in September 1942. The POW camp opened in July 1945. At maximum, it held 1149 German POWs in December 1945.

Tulare, Tulare County, CA (branch camp under Cooke), county fairgrounds. The camp opened in December 1944. This location had been used earlier as a Japanese assembly center. A dental clinic used by several of the branch POW camps in the area was located here. The maximum population was 498 German POWs in December 1945, doing agricultural work. They harvested cotton, vegetables, and fruits. The camp was deactivated in January 1946. As with most camps, the buildings were auctioned off and moved, leaving no trace of the camp.

Tule Lake, Siskiyou County, CA (branch camp under White, OR). Originally this location was a Civilia Conservation Corps camp. The POW camp opened in June 1944. It was set up by 150 Italian POWs who lived in tents while their guards lived in the high school gym in the nearby town of Tulelake. The maximum population was 941 German POWs in October 1944 doing work classified as military, agricultural, and other. The local farmers hired them to clear canals of moss and algae. Today five of the original CCC buildings remain in poor condition. It is now part of the National Park Service's Tule Lake Unit of WWII Valor in the Pacific National Monument.

Upper Jones Tract, San Joaquin County, CA (branch camp under Stockton). The camp opened in May 1945. At maximum, it held 250 German POWs in May 1945, doing agricultural work.

Vernalis, San Joaquin County, CA (branch camp under Stockton). The camp opened in May 1945. The maximum population was 1,770 German POWs in October 1945, doing agricultural work. A German POW, Wilhelm Oellerich, died of meningitis in this location and rumors indicate that his ghost remains here.

Windsor, Sonoma County, CA (branch camp under Beale). The camp opened in August 1944. At maximum, it held 1,236 German POWs in August 1945, doing agricultural work. In June 1946 it was transferred from the War Department to Department of Agriculture.

Death Index

A total of 880 Germans (includes three Russians, four Austrians, one Yugoslavian, one Czech, and one Turk), 172 Italians, twenty-three Japanese (includes one Korean) out of 1,076 POWs who died while held in the US during WWI and WWII. Forty-four men died or were buried in Northern California while POWs.

Assmann, Albert: (born 11 June 1891, died 13 March 1945 in Yuba County, buried at Camp Beale, transferred to Golden Gate National Cemetery, CA). An investigation ruled this death as a suicide.

Behrens, Willi: (born 22 May 1922, died 11 October 1944 in Calaveras River, San Joaquin County; buried at Benicia Arsenal Post Cemetery, CA). He drowned while his group was on a river outing.

Berkemer, Willie: (born 6 February 1920, died 25 May 1945 in Santa Barbara County, buried at Camp Cooke, transferred to Golden Gate National Cemetery, CA). His death was due to bronchitis/pneumonia.

Bethke, Wilhelm: (born 30 September 1901, died 30 March 1946 at San Francisco, buried at Golden Gate National Cemetery, CA). His death was due to stomach cancer.

Boarino, Renato: (born 14 November 1912, died 8 January 1945 in Alameda County, buried at Golden Gate National Cemetery, CA). He died of a pulmonary embolism.

Buccella, Mario: (died 27 May 1945, buried at Camp Cooke, transferred to Golden Gate National Cemetery, CA). His cause of death is shown as hemorrhages, shock.

Carvutto, Pasquale: (born 15 February 1916, died 7 November 1944 in San Mateo County, buried at Golden Gate National Cemetery, CA). He died of septicemia.

Denzel, Johann: (born 23 January 1917, died 30 December 1944 in Yuba County, buried at Camp Beale, buried at Golden Gate National Cemetery, CA). An investigation ruled this death as a suicide.

Deul, Georg: (born 9 July 1908, died 14 March 1946 in Santa Barbara County, buried at Camp Cooke, transferred to Golden Gate National Cemetery, CA). He died of syphilis.

Di Gicia, Santo: (died 20 February 1945, buried at Camp Beale, buried at Golden Gate National Cemetery, CA). He died of echinococcus.

Felgenhauer, Johann: (died 16 October 1945 in Bonneville County, ID; buried at Rupert, ID; transferred to Golden Gate National Cemetery, CA). He died of uremia.

Fisher (Fischer), Hans: (born 24 February 1906, died 25 October 1945 in Stockton, San Joaquin County, buried at Benicia Arsenal Post Cemetery, CA). An investigation ruled this as an accidental death of gastroenteritis.

Gall, Ernst: (born 1 January 1922, died 25 August 1944 at Stockton, San Joaquin County, buried at Benicia Arsenal Post Cemetery, CA). He died of pneumonia.

Giardullo, Vito: (born 1 January 1916, died 22 September 1944 at Camp Lockett in San Diego County, buried at Camp Cooke, transferred to Golden Gate National Cemetery, CA). He died of spinal meningitis.

Giersberg, Josef: (born 14 June 1901, died 1 August 1945 at San Francisco, buried at Golden Gate National Cemetery, CA). He died of pneumonia.

Gori, Luigi: (born 21 April 1921, died 5 November 1945 at San Francisco, buried at Golden Gate National Cemetery, CA). He died of a skull fracture.

Granata, Rosario: (born 2 January 1911, died 31 July 1945 at San Francisco, buried at Golden Gate National Cemetery, CA). He died of a jaw tumor.

Guerrieri, Giovanni: (born 1 January 1908, died 14 December 1945 in Riverside County, buried at Camp Cooke, transferred to Golden Gate National Cemetery, CA). He died of a coronary occlusion.

Hafer, Karl Heinz: (born 9 February 1925, died 6 December 1945 at Stockton, San Joaquin County, buried at Benicia Arsenal Post Cemetery, CA). He died as the result of an electrical accident.

Haussler, Longin: (born 15 February 1915, died 9 November 1945 in Los Angeles County, buried at Camp Cooke, transferred to Golden Gate National Cemetery, CA). He died of a pulmonary thrombus.

Heinze, Arno George: (born 3 July 1910, died 22 August 1945 in Los Angeles County, buried at Camp Cooke, transferred to Golden Gate National Cemetery, CA). He died of diffuse peritonitis.

Hupe, Ernest: (died 9 February 1945, buried at Camp Cooke, transferred to Golden Gate National Cemetery, CA). An investigation ruled this death a suicide.

Knopf, Heinz: (born 1 March 1918, died 15 August 1945 in Tracy, San Joaquin County, buried at Benicia Arsenal Post Cemetery, CA). An investigation ruled this death a suicide.

Kontowski, Erich Paul: (died 23 November 1945 in Twin Falls County, ID; buried at Rupert, ID, transferred to Golden Gate National Cemetery, CA). He died of a coronary occlusion.

Krafthofer, Ernst: (died 21 August 1945, buried at Camp Cooke, transferred to Golden Gate National Cemetery, CA). He died of a skull fracture.

Kuerschner, Wolfgang: (born 4 August 1921, died 1 February 1946 in Yuba County, buried at Camp Beale, transferred to Golden Gate National Cemetery, CA). He died of a cerebral embolism.

Maierhofer, Georg: (died 24 August 1945 in Monterey County, buried at Camp Cooke, transferred to Golden Gate National Cemetery, CA). He died of leptomeningitis.

Mangold, Richard: (born 17 September 1922, died 3 December 1945 in Monterey County, buried at Camp Cooke, transferred to Golden Gate National Cemetery, CA). He died of gunshot wounds.

Mattick, Walter: (born 9 April 1919, died 27 February 1946 in Santa Barbara County, buried at Camp Cooke, transferred to Golden Gate National Cemetery, CA). He died of lymphosarcoma.

Mattner, Werner: (born 8 November 1922, died 16 September 1945 in Stockton, San Joaquin County, buried at Benicia Arsenal Post Cemetery, CA. An investigation ruled this death a suicide.

Morretti, Tarcisio: (died 25 June 1944 and buried at Benicia Arsenal Post Cemetery, CA). He died of typhoid fever.

Nedbal, Otto: (died 3 December 1945 in Minidoka County, ID; buried at Rupert, ID, transferred to Golden Gate National Cemetery, CA). He died of coronary thrombosis.

Nedell, Wilhelm: (died 19 June 1946 at Burley, ID; buried at Rupert, ID, transferred to Golden Gate National Cemetery, CA). He died of a ruptured spleen.

Neuhaus, Richard: (born 3 January 1921, died 6 December 1945 at Stockton, San Joaquin County, buried at Benicia Arsenal Post Cemetery, CA). He died of an electrical shock.

Oellerich, Wilhelm F.: (born 28 November 1894, died 26 October 1945 in Stanislaus County, buried at Golden Gate National Cemetery, CA). He died of meningitis. It is rumored that his ghost still haunts the remains of the POW camp at Vernalis.

Palmarini, Giorgio: (born 21 January 1915, died 15 February 1945 in San Bernardino County, buried at Camp Cooke, transferred to Golden Gate National Cemetery, CA). He died of a heart rupture and fractures.

Pellino, Vincenzo: (born 17 January 1909, died 9 July 1944 in Lassen County, buried at Camp Beale, transferred to Golden Gate National Cemetery, CA). An investigation ruled his death a suicide.

Riggi, Niccolo: (born 9 May 1913, died 9 February 1945 in Lassen County, buried at Camp Beale, transferred to Golden Gate National Cemetery, CA). He died of hemorrhages during a tonsillectomy.

Rosenberger, Hubert: (died 14 January 1946, buried at Camp Cooke, transferred to Golden Gate National Cemetery, CA). He died of meningitis.

Schmidt, Paul Rudi: (died 14 September 1944 at Pocatello, ID; buried at Rupert, ID, transferred to Golden Gate National Cemetery, CA). He died of a pulmonary embolism.

Starke, Alfred: (born 15 May 1909, died 20 November 1945 in McClellan, Sacramento County, buried at Benicia Arsenal Post Cemetery, CA). He died of bacterial endocarditis.

Van Radecke, Herbert: (born 21 February 1915, died 25 August 1945 at San Francisco, buried at Golden Gate National Cemetery, CA). An investigation ruled this death a suicide.

Wagner, Alfred: (born 8 November 1922, died 15 December 1945 at San Francisco, buried at Golden Gate National Cemetery, CA). He died of a brain tumor.

Wude, Henrich: (died 30 October 1944 in Minidoka County, ID; buried at Rupert, ID, transferred to Golden Gate National Cemetery, CA). He died of an intestinal obstruction.

Burial Locations List

A total of ninety-one US Military and civilian cemeteries contained POW burials in the United States.

Place of Burial (in Northern California):

Benicia Arsenal Post Cemetery, CA, now in the care of the National Park Service. This cemetery contains one Italian and eight German WWII POW burials.
Camp Beale, CA, now Beale AFB, an active military installation. (three German and three Italian WWII POW burials transferred to Golden Gate National Cemetery).
Golden Gate National Cemetery, San Bruno, CA. This cemetery contains five German and four Italian POW burials, plus those transferred from Beale (six), Cooke (fourteen), and Idaho (six). No Japanese POW burials occurred in California.

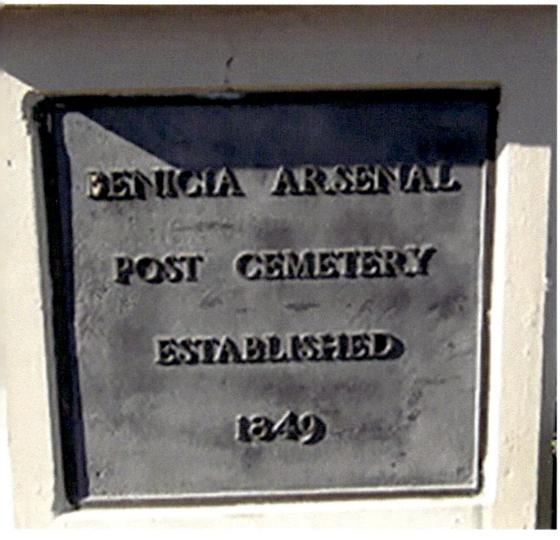

Above left: Benicia Arsenal Post Cemetery, Benicia, CA. [*Image from www.findagrave.com*]

Above right: Golden Gate National Cemetery, San Bruno, CA. [*Image from www.cem.va.gov/cems/nchp/goldengate.asp*]

Appendix A

POW Labor

PRISONERS OF WAR WORK

CLOTHING AND EQUIPMENT

FORT MEADE, MD.

CAMP BLANDING, FLA.

FORT McCLELLAN, ALA.

CAMP BRECKINRIDGE, KY.

FORT OGELTHORPE, GA.

CAMP CARSON, COLO.

WD – ASF – PMGO

MAN-MONTHS SUMMARY OF PRISONER-OF-WAR LABOR

A man-months (strength) summary
to paid work, and type of work performed, a
are for all prisoners in the United States
medical institutions, and Hawaii. Man-mon
oners at work are calculated by dividing t
number of workdays in the month. These m
for the month.

MAN-MONTHS OF PRISONER-OF-WAR
NOVEMBER AND DECEMBER 194

Item
AVAILABILITY AND ASSIGNMENT
TOTAL MAN-MONTHS a/ . . . .
NOT AVAILABLE FOR PAID WORK . . . .
AVAILABLE FOR PAID WORK . . . .
Not Assigned to Work . . . .
Assigned to Work . . . .
Work Stoppage b/ . . . .
Worked Full Time . . . .
TYPE OF PAID WORK
TOTAL MAN-MONTHS . . . .
Prisoner-of-War Camp Work . . . .
Army Post, Camp, and Station Work . . .
Contract Work . . . .

a/ Calculated from total man-days. Exclude
and medical institutions, and the Territ
b/ Average number of men assigned to work
bad weather, non-use by contract employe

MAN-MONTHS AVAILABLE F
DONE BY PRI

LABOR AVAILABILITY AND ASSIGNMENT

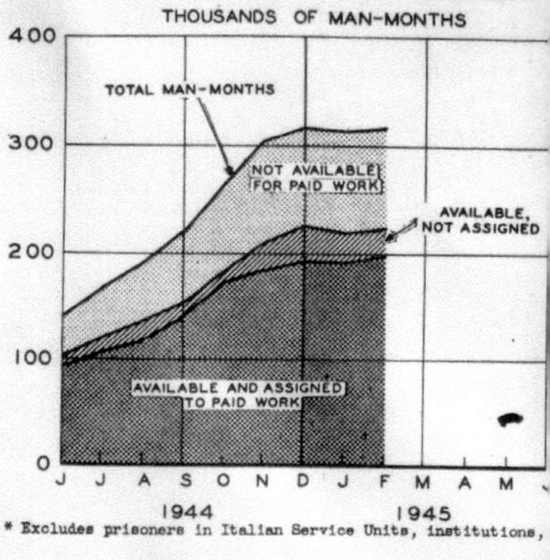

* Excludes prisoners in Italian Service Units, institutions,

42

POW Work images provided by PMGO, located at NARA College Park, MD, RG 389

ner-of-war labor availability, assignment
in the table and chart below. These data
those in Italian Service Units, penal and
risoners available for paid work and pris-
. number of man-days so reported by the
data represent average prisoner strength

BY TYPE OF WORK AND BY MONTH,
NUARY AND FEBRUARY 1945

	Dec 1944	Jan 1945	Feb 1945
	318,034	316,824	318,562
	89,862	95,806	95,681
	228,172	221,018	222,881
	34,392	30,074	23,819
	193,780	190,944	199,062
	22,020	19,139	18,559
	171,760	171,805	180,503
	171,760	171,805	180,503
	28,975	27,810	28,090
	96,915	102,831	112,711
	45,870	41,164	39,702

rs of war in Italian Service Units, penal
waii.
each workday during the month because of
her temporary causes of work stoppage.

BOR, AND TYPE OF WORK
S OF WAR*

TYPE OF WORK PERFORMED
THOUSANDS OF MAN-MONTHS

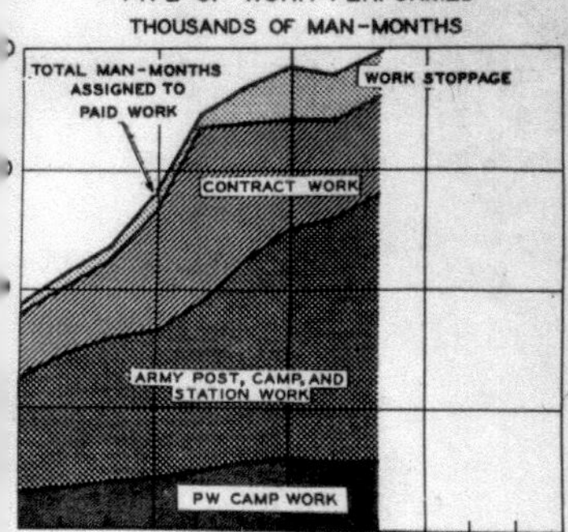

RESTRICTED

PRISONERS OF WAR WORK

MOTOR MAINTENANCE

FT. DIX, N. J.

FORT ROBINSON, NEB.

FORT KNOX, KY.

FORT DIX, N. J.

CAMP CAMPBELL, KY.

FT. BRAGG, N. C.

WD - ASF - PMGO

PRISONERS OF WAR WORK

REPAIRS AND UTILITIES

FOLLOWING LIST OF SUGGESTED REPAIRS AND UTILITIES OCCUPATIONS FOR PRISONERS OF WAR WAS PREPARED BY OFFICE OF THE CHIEF OF ENGINEERS

SPECIFICATION NUMBER (TM-12-427) OCCUPATION

CAMP CLARK, MO.

FORT OGELTHORPE, GA.

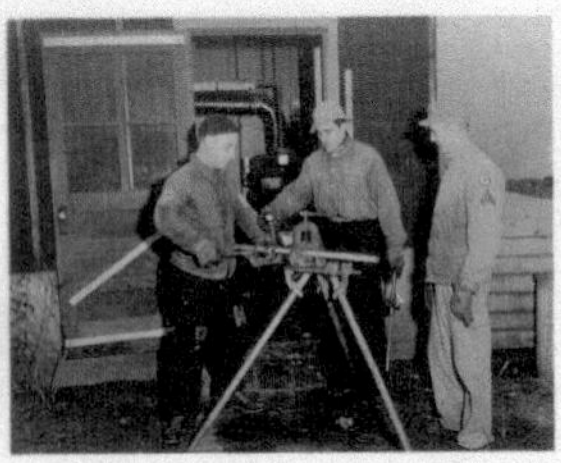

CAMP CLARK, MO.

FORT LEONARD WOOD, MO.

WD - ASF - PMGO

TAILOR, CLOTHING REPAIR SHOP

COBBLERS, SHOE REPAIR SHOP

MECHANIC, TYPEWRITER REPAIR SHOP

POW Work images provided by PMGO, located at NARA College Park, MD, RG 389

OCCUPATIONS AND SKILLS OF

PRISONERS OF WAR

.to body repairmen
.to painters
to mechanics
'tists
kers, bread and pastry
Mixers
Oven operators
Moulders
Dividers
rbers
acksmiths
okkeepers
ot and shoe repairmen
xmakers
icklayers
ushmen
lldozer operators
tchers
binetmakers
nvas workers
rpenters
Bench
Car
Concrete form
House
Rough
r washers and greasers
ment and concrete
inishers
ramic workers
eckers
emists
Sewage disposal plant
eaners
Engine
Floor
Machine
erks
General office
Statistical
Stock
othing classifiers
othing repairmen
al handlers
bblers
untermen
ncrete workers
nstruction machinery
perators
nstruction laborers
oks
EM mess
Officers' mess
PX restaurant
ppersmiths
anemen
aters
irymen
ntal lab. workers
tch diggers
aftsmen
agline operators
ers
ectrical repairmen

Electricians
Auto
House
Motor
Radio
Engravers
Fan cleaners
Farm hands
Farm machinery operators
Firemen
Boiler and furnace
Fire department
Form builders
Flashlight repairmen
Freight handlers
Furnace cleaners
Furnace tenders
Furniture repairmen
Foundry workers
Garbage laborers
Garbage collectors
Gardners
Glaziers
Goldsmiths
Graders and packers
Fruit and vegetable
Grass mowers
Grave diggers
Greenhouse workers
Grounds keepers
Harness makers
Harvest hands
Cotton
Fruit
General
Sugar beets
Sugarcane
Tobacco
Vegetable
Hospital orderlies
Incinerator operators
Insect exterminators
Interpreters
Instrument repairmen
Irrigation workers
Janitors
Jewelers
Kitchen police
Laborer, general
Language teachers
Latrine orderlies
Laundry workers
Checker
Marker
Presser
Sorter
Washer
Leather workers
Locksmiths
Lumberyard workers
Machinists
Masons
Meatcutters
Mechanics

OCCUPATIONS AND SKILLS OF

PRISONERS OF WAR (Continued)

Maintenance workers:
Ditches
Grounds
Powerline right-of-way
Railroad right-of-way
Roads and streets
Septic tanks
Model and pattern makers
Molders
Motor repairmen
Electrical
Gasoline and diesel
Nurserymen
Office-machine repairmen
Oilers
Orthopedic aids
Painters
Construction
Maintenance
Vehicle
Paper balers
Photograph finishers
Photographers' assistants
Physicians
Piano tuners
Pinboys
Plasterers
Printers
Plumbers
Poultry dressers
Pulpwood cutters
Quarry workers
Radio repairmen
Ration breakdown workers
Repairmen
Automobile
Clothing
Electrical
Furniture
Instrument
Motor
Office machine
Radio
Road equipment
Shoe
Tent
Tire
Typewriter
Watch
Railroad maintenance
workers
Refrigeration mechanics
Road equipment repairmen
Roofers
Salvage workers:
Building materials
Clothing and equipment
Electrical equipment
Motors
Paper
Saw filers
Sawmill workers
Scrubmen
Servicemen, motor pool
Sheet metal workers

Sewage disposal plant
operators
Shoe classifiers
Shoe repairmen
Sign painters
Silversmiths
Spray operators
Mosquito control
Tree spraying
Stablemen
Steam cleaners
Vehicles
Steam fitters
Stonecutters
Stone masons
Storekeepers
Sweepers
Tailors
Teachers
Teamsters
Telephone linemen
Tent repairmen
Textile balers
Tile setters
Timekeepers
Tinsmiths
Tire changers
Tire repairmen
Tool checkers and sorters
Tool dressers and
sharpeners
Track repairmen
Tree fellers
Tractor drivers
Truck drivers
Type setters
Typewriter repairmen
Typists
Upholsterers
Furniture
Vehicles
Veterinarians
Waiters
EM mess
Officers' club
PX restaurant
Ward boys
Station hospital
Warehousemen
Post ordnance
Post quartermaster
Salvage shop
Post exchange
Private industry
Wash-rack man
Watch repairmen
Water plant operators
Weavers
Basketry
Webbing repairmen
Welders
Woodsmen
Wood workers
X-ray lab. technicians
Yardmen

MECHANICS, VEHICLE REPAIR SHOP

AUTO PAINTER, VEHICLE REPAIR SHOP

PLUMBERS, POST PLUMBING SHOP

PRISONERS OF WAR WORK

POST ENGINEER WORK

CAMP TRINIDAD, COLO.

CAMP SHELBY, MISS.

FORT LEONARD WOOD, MO.

CAMP BRECKINRIDGE, KY.

CAMP BRECKINRIDGE, KY.

CAMP WHEELER, GA.

WD - ASF - PMGO

PRISONER

POST EN

CAMP CLINTON, MISS.

EDGEWOOD ARSENAL, MD.

GALVESTON AAB, TEX.

POW Work images provided by PMGO, located at NARA College Park, MD, RG 389

WAR WORK

EER WORK

CAMP SUTTON, N. C.

CAMP CARSON, COLO.

FORT LEONARD WOOD, MO.

- PMGO

PRISONERS OF WAR WORK

POST ENGINEER WORK

FORT BENJAMIN HARRISON, IND.

CAMP BRECKINRIDGE, KY.

NORFOLK ARMY AIR BASE, VA.

CAMP CLINTON, MISS.

FORT DEVENS, MASS.

CAMP LEE, VA.

WD - ASF - PMGO

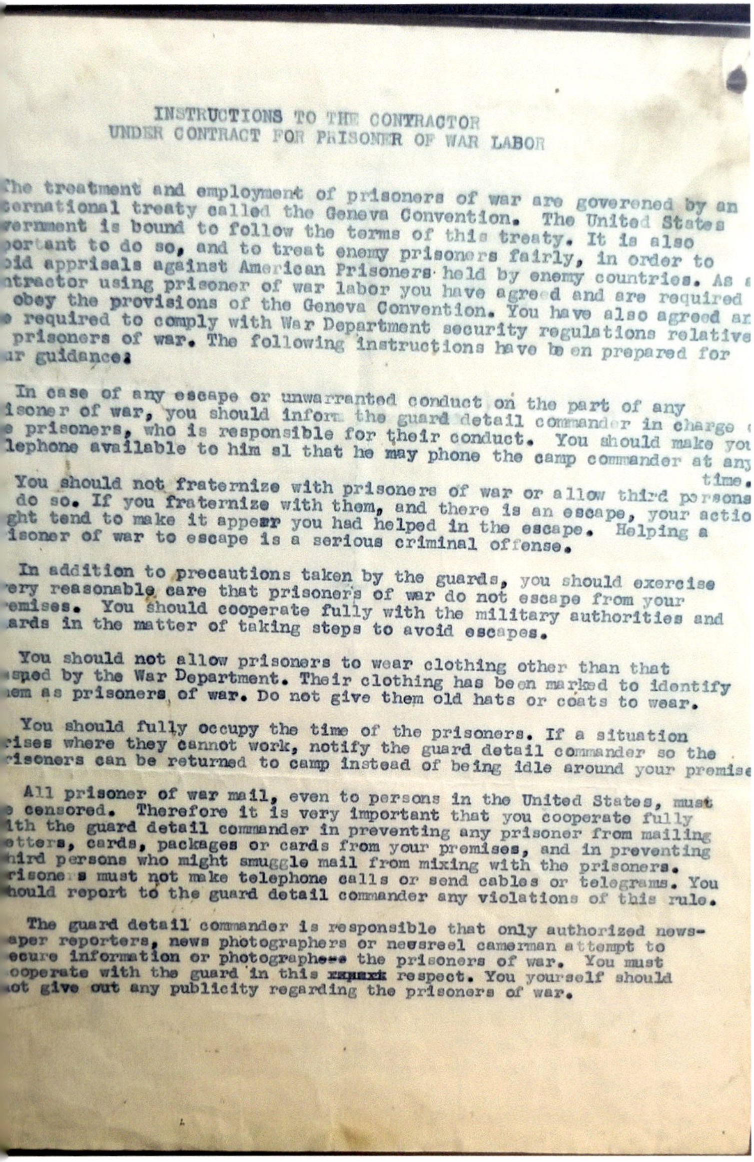

INSTRUCTIONS TO THE CONTRACTOR
UNDER CONTRACT FOR PRISONER OF WAR LABOR

he treatment and employment of prisoners of war are governed by an ernational treaty called the Geneva Convention. The United States vernment is bound to follow the terms of this treaty. It is also portant to do so, and to treat enemy prisoners fairly, in order to oid apprisals against American Prisoners held by enemy countries. As a ntractor using prisoner of war labor you have agreed and are required obey the provisions of the Geneva Convention. You have also agreed ar e required to comply with War Department security regulations relative prisoners of war. The following instructions have been prepared for ur guidance:

In case of any escape or unwarranted conduct on the part of any isoner of war, you should inform the guard detail commander in charge e prisoners, who is responsible for their conduct. You should make you lephone available to him sl that he may phone the camp commander at any time.

You should not fraternize with prisoners of war or allow third persons do so. If you fraternize with them, and there is an escape, your actio ght tend to make it appear you had helped in the escape. Helping a isoner of war to escape is a serious criminal offense.

In addition to precautions taken by the guards, you should exercise ery reasonable care that prisoner's of war do not escape from your emises. You should cooperate fully with the military authorities and ards in the matter of taking steps to avoid escapes.

You should not allow prisoners to wear clothing other than that ssued by the War Department. Their clothing has been marked to identify em as prisoners of war. Do not give them old hats or coats to wear.

You should fully occupy the time of the prisoners. If a situation rises where they cannot work, notify the guard detail commander so the risoners can be returned to camp instead of being idle around your premise

All prisoner of war mail, even to persons in the United States, must e censored. Therefore it is very important that you cooperate fully ith the guard detail commander in preventing any prisoner from mailing etters, cards, packages or cards from your premises, and in preventing hird persons who might smuggle mail from mixing with the prisoners. risoners must not make telephone calls or send cables or telegrams. You hould report to the guard detail commander any violations of this rule.

The guard detail commander is responsible that only authorized newsaper reporters, news photographers or newsreel cameraman attempt to ecure information or photographees the prisoners of war. You must ooperate with the guard in this xxxxxx respect. You yourself should ot give out any publicity regarding the prisoners of war.

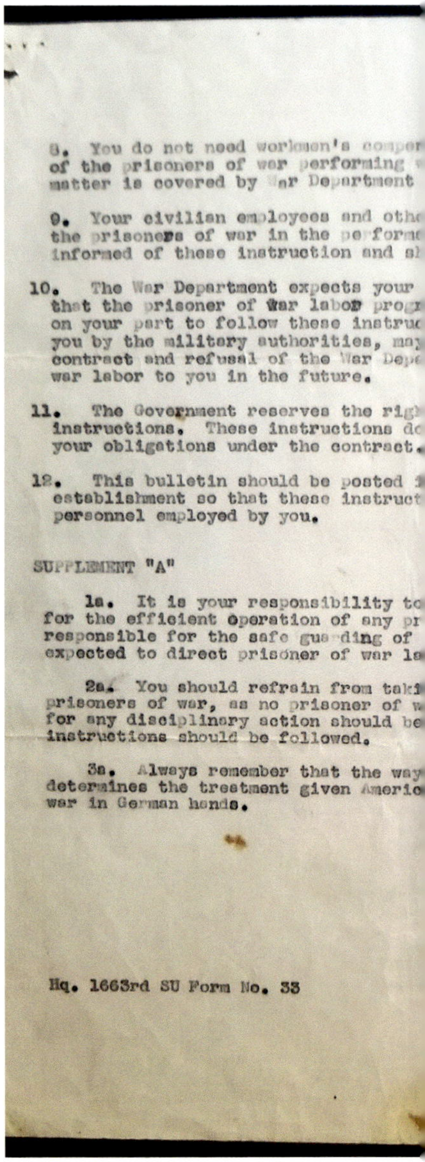

8. You do not need workmen's compen of the prisoners of war performing matter is covered by War Department

9. Your civilian employees and othe the prisoners of war in the perform informed of these instruction and sh

10. The War Department expects your that the prisoner of war labor progr on your part to follow these instruc you by the military authorities, may contract and refusal of the War Depa war labor to you in the future.

11. The Government reserves the righ instructions. These instructions do your obligations under the contract.

12. This bulletin should be posted i establishment so that these instruct personnel employed by you.

SUPPLEMENT "A"

1a. It is your responsibility to for the efficient operation of any pr responsible for the safe guarding of expected to direct prisoner of war la

2a. You should refrain from taki prisoners of war, as no prisoner of w for any disciplinary action should be instructions should be followed.

3a. Always remember that the way determines the treatment given Americ war in German hands.

Hq. 1663rd SU Form No. 33

POW contract instructions, courtesy of Gary Reeves collection of POW artifacts

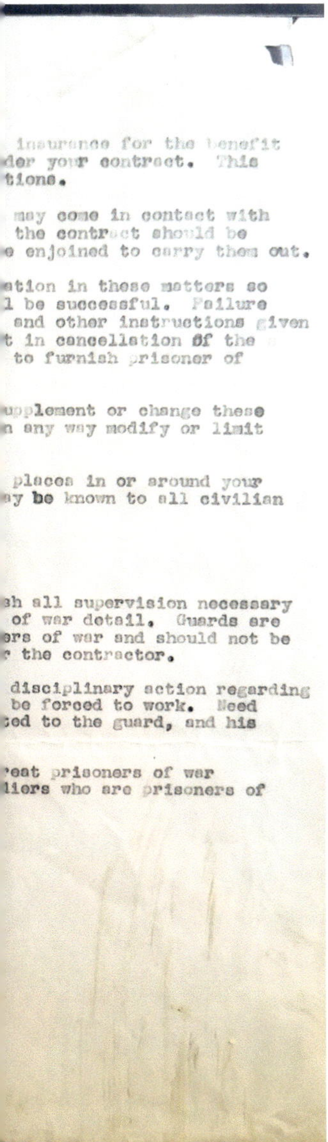

insurance for the benefit
der your contract. This
tions.

may come in contact with
the contract should be
e enjoined to carry them out.

ation in these matters so
l be successful. Failure
and other instructions given
t in cancellation of the
to furnish prisoner of

upplement or change these
n any way modify or limit

places in or around your
ay be known to all civilian

sh all supervision necessary
of war detail. Guards are
ers of war and should not be
r the contractor.

disciplinary action regarding
be forced to work. Need
sed to the guard, and his

reat prisoners of war
liers who are prisoners of

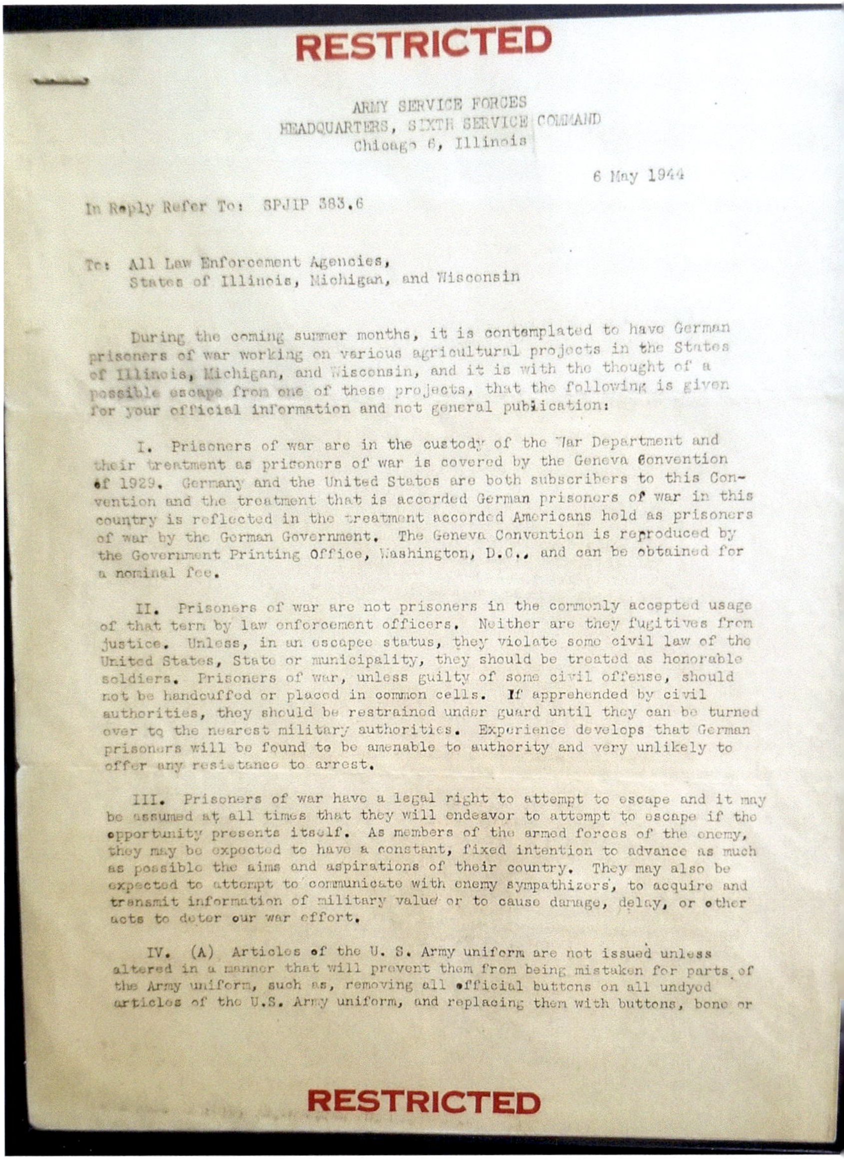

RESTRICTED

ARMY SERVICE FORCES
HEADQUARTERS, SIXTH SERVICE COMMAND
Chicago 6, Illinois

6 May 1944

In Reply Refer To: SPJIP 383.6

To: All Law Enforcement Agencies,
States of Illinois, Michigan, and Wisconsin

During the coming summer months, it is contemplated to have German prisoners of war working on various agricultural projects in the States of Illinois, Michigan, and Wisconsin, and it is with the thought of a possible escape from one of these projects, that the following is given for your official information and not general publication:

I. Prisoners of war are in the custody of the War Department and their treatment as prisoners of war is covered by the Geneva Convention of 1929. Germany and the United States are both subscribers to this Convention and the treatment that is accorded German prisoners of war in this country is reflected in the treatment accorded Americans held as prisoners of war by the German Government. The Geneva Convention is reproduced by the Government Printing Office, Washington, D.C., and can be obtained for a nominal fee.

II. Prisoners of war are not prisoners in the commonly accepted usage of that term by law enforcement officers. Neither are they fugitives from justice. Unless, in an escapee status, they violate some civil law of the United States, State or municipality, they should be treated as honorable soldiers. Prisoners of war, unless guilty of some civil offense, should not be handcuffed or placed in common cells. If apprehended by civil authorities, they should be restrained under guard until they can be turned over to the nearest military authorities. Experience develops that German prisoners will be found to be amenable to authority and very unlikely to offer any resistance to arrest.

III. Prisoners of war have a legal right to attempt to escape and it may be assumed at all times that they will endeavor to attempt to escape if the opportunity presents itself. As members of the armed forces of the enemy, they may be expected to have a constant, fixed intention to advance as much as possible the aims and aspirations of their country. They may also be expected to attempt to communicate with enemy sympathizers, to acquire and transmit information of military value or to cause damage, delay, or other acts to deter our war effort.

IV. (A) Articles of the U. S. Army uniform are not issued unless altered in a manner that will prevent them from being mistaken for parts of the Army uniform, such as, removing all official buttons on all undyed articles of the U.S. Army uniform, and replacing them with buttons, bone or

RESTRICTED

POW labor in Sixth Service Command. [*Courtesy of Gary Reeves collection of POW artifacts*]

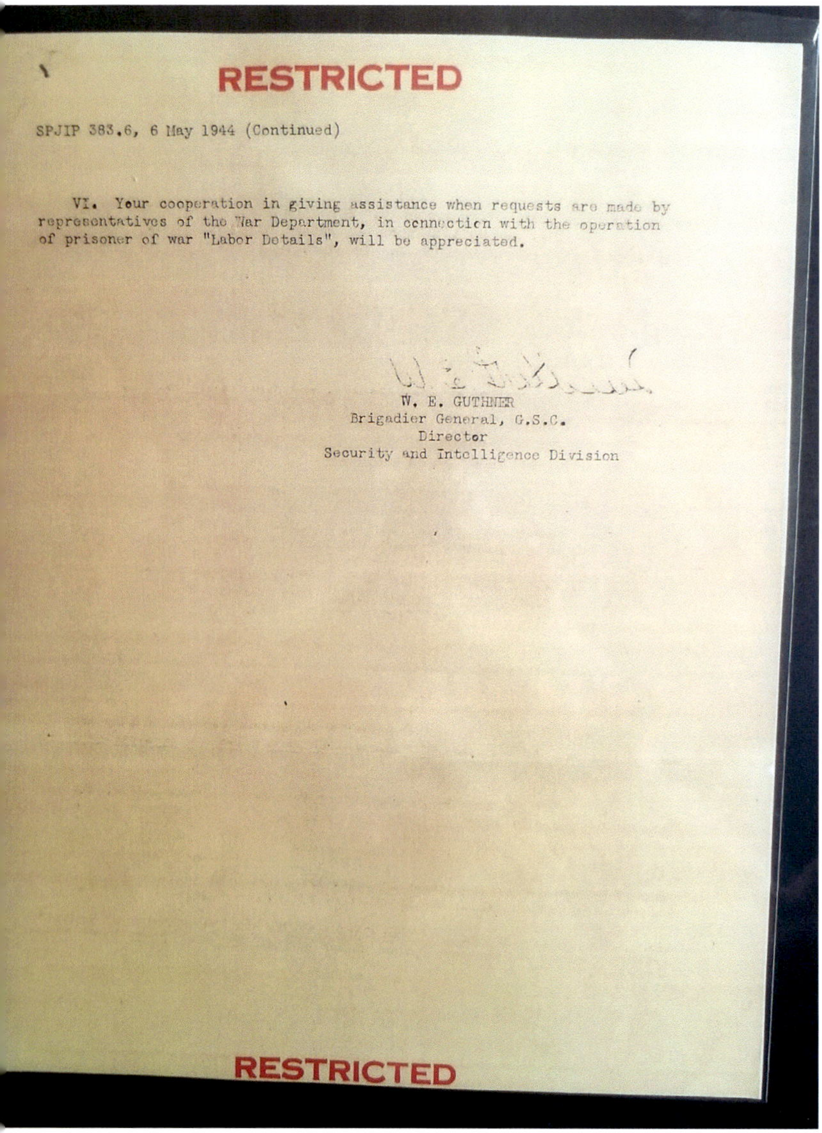

RESTRICTED

SPJIP 383.6, 6 May 1944 (Continued)

VI. Your cooperation in giving assistance when requests are made by representatives of the War Department, in connection with the operation of prisoner of war "Labor Details", will be appreciated.

W. E. GUTHNER
Brigadier General, G.S.C.
Director
Security and Intelligence Division

RESTRICTED

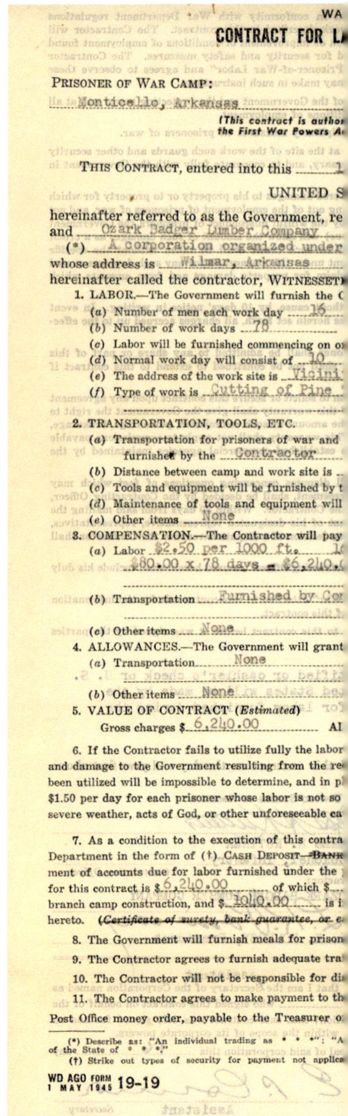

WA

CONTRACT FOR L

PRISONER OF WAR CAMP:

Monticello, Arkansas

(This contract is author
the First War Powers A

THIS CONTRACT, entered into this 1

UNITED S

hereinafter referred to as the Government, re
and Ozark Badger Lumber Company
(*) A corporation organized under
whose address is Wilmar, Arkansas
hereinafter called the contractor, WITNESSETH

1. LABOR.—The Government will furnish the
(a) Number of men each work day 16
(b) Number of work days 78
(c) Labor will be furnished commencing on o
(d) Normal work day will consist of 10
(e) The address of the work site is Vicini
(f) Type of work is Cutting of Pine

2. TRANSPORTATION, TOOLS, ETC.
(a) Transportation for prisoners of war and furnished by the Contractor
(b) Distance between camp and work site is
(c) Tools and equipment will be furnished by t
(d) Maintenance of tools and equipment will
(e) Other items None

3. COMPENSATION.—The Contractor will pay
(a) Labor $2.50 per 1000 ft. 1
$80.00 x 78 days = $6,240.
(b) Transportation Furnished by Co
(c) Other items None

4. ALLOWANCES.—The Government will grant
(a) Transportation None
(b) Other items None

5. VALUE OF CONTRACT (*Estimated*)
Gross charges $ 6,240.00 Al

6. If the Contractor fails to utilize fully the labor
and damage to the Government resulting from the re
been utilized will be impossible to determine, and in p
$1.50 per day for each prisoner whose labor is not so
severe weather, acts of God, or other unforeseeable ca

7. As a condition to the execution of this contra
Department in the form of (†) CASH DEPOSIT—~~BANK~~
ment of accounts due for labor furnished under the
for this contract is $ 6,240.00 of which $
branch camp construction, and $ 1040.00 is i
hereto. ~~(*Certificate of surety, bank guarantee, or c*~~

8. The Government will furnish meals for prison

9. The Contractor agrees to furnish adequate tra

10. The Contractor will not be responsible for di

11. The Contractor agrees to make payment to th
Post Office money order, payable to the Treasurer o

(*) Describe as: "An individual trading as * * *"; "A
of the State of * * *."
(†) Strike out types of security for payment not applica

WD AGO FORM 19-19
1 MAY 1945

POW labor in Sixth Service Command. [*Courtesy of Gary Reeves collection of POW artifacts*]

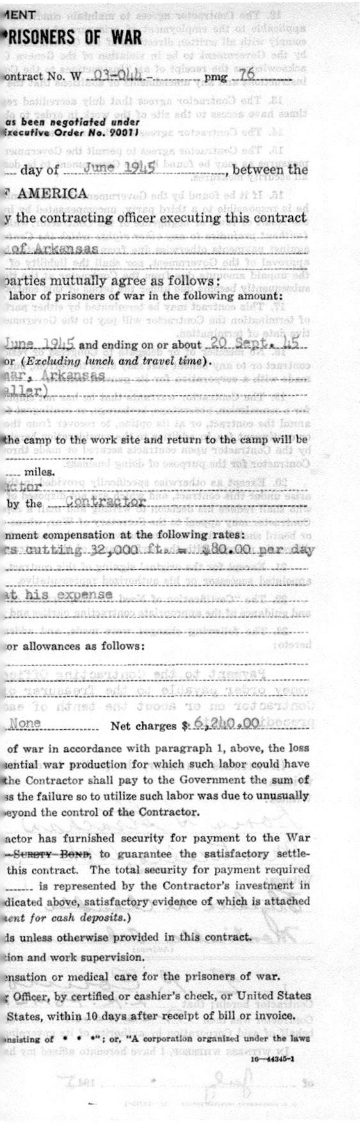

MENT

PRISONERS OF WAR

ontract No. W 03-044- pmg 76

as been negotiated under
Executive Order No. 9001)

day of June 1945, between the

AMERICA

y the contracting officer executing this contract

of Arkansas

parties mutually agree as follows:

labor of prisoners of war in the following amount:

June 1945 and ending on or about 20 Sept. 45

or (Excluding lunch and travel time).

nar, Arkansas

aller)

the camp to the work site and return to the camp will be

miles.

actor

by the Contractor

nment compensation at the following rates:

rs cutting 32,000 ft. = $80.00 per day

at his expense

or allowances as follows:

None Net charges $ 6240.00

of war in accordance with paragraph 1, above, the loss
sential war production for which such labor could have
the Contractor shall pay to the Government the sum of
ss the failure so to utilize such labor was due to unusually
beyond the control of the Contractor.

actor has furnished security for payment to the War
~~Surety Bond~~, to guarantee the satisfactory settle-
this contract. The total security for payment required
...... is represented by the Contractor's investment in
dicated above, satisfactory evidence of which is attached
ent for cash deposits.)

ds unless otherwise provided in this contract.

tion and work supervision.

ensation or medical care for the prisoners of war.

g Officer, by certified or cashier's check, or United States
States, within 10 days after receipt of bill or invoice.

onsisting of " " "; or, "A corporation organized under the laws

16—44345-1

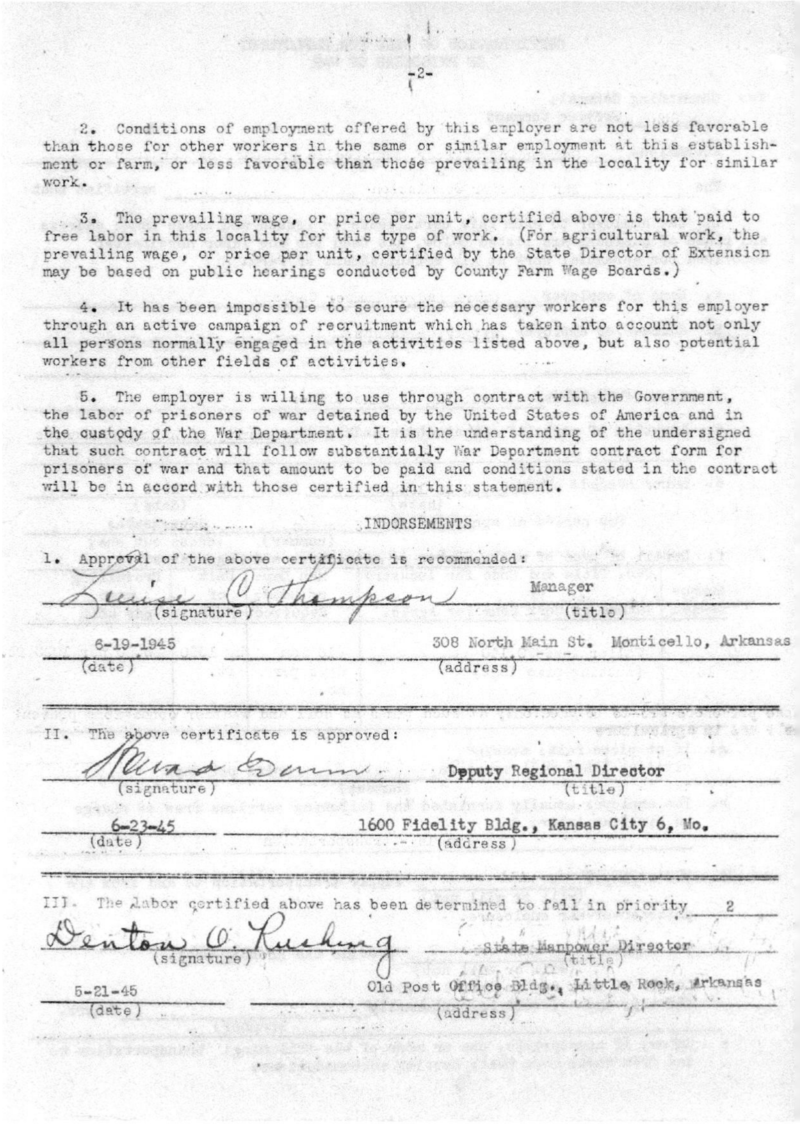

-2-

2. Conditions of employment offered by this employer are not less favorable than those for other workers in the same or similar employment at this establishment or farm, or less favorable than those prevailing in the locality for similar work.

3. The prevailing wage, or price per unit, certified above is that paid to free labor in this locality for this type of work. (For agricultural work, the prevailing wage, or price per unit, certified by the State Director of Extension may be based on public hearings conducted by County Farm Wage Boards.)

4. It has been impossible to secure the necessary workers for this employer through an active campaign of recruitment which has taken into account not only all persons normally engaged in the activities listed above, but also potential workers from other fields of activities.

5. The employer is willing to use through contract with the Government, the labor of prisoners of war detained by the United States of America and in the custody of the War Department. It is the understanding of the undersigned that such contract will follow substantially War Department contract form for prisoners of war and that amount to be paid and conditions stated in the contract will be in accord with those certified in this statement.

INDORSEMENTS

1. Approval of the above certificate is recommended:

Louise C. Thompson (signature) — Manager (title)

6-19-1945 (date) — 308 North Main St. Monticello, Arkansas (address)

II. The above certificate is approved:

Nevada Dunn (signature) — Deputy Regional Director (title)

6-23-45 (date) — 1600 Fidelity Bldg., Kansas City 6, Mo. (address)

III. The labor certified above has been determined to fall in priority 2

Denton O. Rushing (signature) — State Manpower Director (title)

5-21-45 (date) — Old Post Office Bldg., Little Rock, Arkansas (address)

Work contracts for civilians to obtain POW labor. [*Courtesy of Michael Pomeroy*]

CERTIFICATION OF NEED FOR EMPLOYMENT
OF PRISONERS OF WAR

To: Commanding General,
8th Service Command

Attention: Commanding Officer, Monticello Prisoner of War Camp

The War Manpower Commission certifies that:

1. The employer to whom this certificate is issued and whose name, address and place of business are listed below, has need for the labor hereinafter described for essential work at his establishment or farm.

a. Name of employer Ozark Badger Lumber Company

b. Address of employer Wilmar, Arkansas

c. Type of business cutting of pine timber

d. Location of work (if not at above address) vicinity of Wilmar, Arkansas

e. Labor needed: From 6-20-1945 (date) to 9-20-1945 (date)

For period of approximately 3 months (number) ~~days~~-months (cross out one)

f. Detail of type of work, number of prisoners, and wage rates:

Number needed	Occ. Title and Code for Industry or Nature of Work Done for Agric.	Man Days or Hours Required	Unit of Work	Prevailing wage per unit
16	Faller - 6-30.140 (cutting pine logs)	416 man days per mo.	by 1000 ft.	$2.50 per 1000 ft.

These prisoners are to be used only at such times as soil and weather conditions prevent their use in agriculture

g. If at piece rate, average civilian labor will complete 2 to 3 (number) units per day.

h. The employer usually furnished the following services free of charge to civilian labor: *
tools - transportation

i. The employer will (will or will not) supply transportation to and from the prisoner-of-war enclosure.

j. The employer will not (will or will not) provide the noonday meal.

k. Length of work day in this locality for this type of work is customarily 8 (number) hours.

* Enter, if appropriate, one or more of the following: transportation to and from work; noon meal; housing accommodations.

Work contracts for civilians to obtain POW labor. [*Courtesy of Michael Pomeroy*]

12. The Contractor agrees to maintain conditions of employment in conformity with War Department regulations applicable to the employment of prisoners of war on the type of work described in this contract. The Contractor will comply with all written directions of the Government for the correction or improvement of conditions of employment found by the Government to be in violation of the Geneva Convention and for security and safety measures. The Contractor acknowledges the receipt of an "Instructions to the Contractor for Prisoner-of-War Labor" and agrees to observe these instructions and any amendments or additions that the Government may make in such instructions.

13. The Contractor agrees that duly accredited representatives of the Government and the protecting power will at all times have access to the site of the work in order to observe the conditions of employment.

14. The Contractor agrees that he has no authority to impose disciplinary measures on prisoners of war.

15. The Contractor agrees to permit the Government to maintain at the site of the work such guards and other security measures as may be found by the Government to be desirable or necessary, and to cooperate fully with the Government in all security measures.

16. If it be found by the Government that the Contractor has suffered damages to his property or to property for which he is responsible to a third party, uncompensated by insurance, arising out of the employment of prisoners of war, and not the result of fault or negligence of the Contractor, which are caused by the willful misconduct of prisoners, the Government (*without prejudice to any other rights which the Contractor may have*) will allow the amount of such damages as a credit against payments otherwise due from the Contractor hereunder; but no such credit shall be taken without the specific approval of the Government, nor shall the liability of the Government under this paragraph for any such damages exceed the unpaid amounts due from the Contractor at the time he files a claim for property damage and from amounts which subsequently become due under the terms of this contract.

17. This contract may be terminated by either party, with or without cause, by 10 days' notice in writing. In event of termination the Contractor will pay to the Government, at the rates herein set forth, all charges accrued up to the effective date of termination.

18. No member of or delegate to Congress or resident commissioner shall be admitted to any share or part of this contract or to any benefit that may arise therefrom, but this provision shall not be construed to extend to this contract if made with a corporation for its general benefit.

19. The Contractor warrants that he has not employed any person to solicit or secure this contract upon any agreement for a commission, percentage, brokerage, or contingent fee. Breach of this warranty shall give the Government the right to annul the contract, or at its option, to recover from the Contractor the amount of such commission, percentage, brokerage, or contingent fee, in addition to the consideration herein set forth. This warranty shall not apply to commissions payable by the Contractor upon contracts secured or made through bona fide established commercial agencies maintained by the Contractor for the purpose of doing business.

20. Except as otherwise specifically provided in this contract, all disputes concerning questions of fact which may arise under this contract, and which are not disposed of by mutual agreement, shall be decided by the Contracting Officer, who shall reduce his decision to writing and mail a copy thereof to the Contractor. Within 30 days from said mailing the Contractor may appeal to the Secretary of War, whose decision or that of his designated representative, representatives, or board shall be final and conclusive upon the parties hereto. Pending decision of a dispute hereunder the Contractor shall diligently proceed with the performance of this contract.

21. Except for the original signing of this contract, the term "Contracting Officer" as used herein shall include his duly appointed successor or his authorized representative.

22. The "Certification of Need for Employment of Prisoners of War" attached to this contract is for the information and guidance of the appropriate contracting parties and is not a part of this contract.

23. The following changes were made, and addenda attached, to this contract before it was signed by the parties hereto:

Payment to the Contracting Officer by certified or cashier's check or U. S. money order payable to the Treasurer of the United States will be made by the Contractor on or about the tenth of each month for labor furnished during the preceding month.

In witness whereof, the parties hereto have executed this contract on the day and year first above written.

Witness: Doris H. Strachan
Monticello Ark
(Address)

The United States of America:
By Jas H Kuttner
JAMES H. KUTTNER
Colonel, Infantry
Contracting Officer.

Witness: Elizabeth W Chandler
Monticello Arkansas
(Address)

Contractor:
OZARK BADGER LUMBER COMPANY
By L. K. Pomeroy
L. K. POMEROY, President.

I, E. P. Connor, certify that I am the Assistant Secretary of the Corporation named as Contractor herein; that L. K. Pomeroy who signed this contract on behalf of the Contractor was then President of said Corporation; that said contract was duly signed for and on behalf of said Corporation by authority of its governing body and is within the scope of its corporate powers.

In witness whereof, I have hereunto affixed my hand and the seal of said corporation this 16 day of July, 1945

E. P. Connor
Assistant *Secretary.*

U. S. GOVERNMENT PRINTING OFFICE 16—44345-1

Work contracts for civilians to obtain POW labor. [*Courtesy of Michael Pomeroy*]

Appendix B

Museums and Websites

Arizona Historical Society Museum, Papago Park, AZ - www.arizonahistoricalsociety.org/museums

Billion Graves—www.billiongraves.com

Bureau of Land Management, Needles, CA at www.blm.gov/tag/needles-field-office

California Military Museum—www.militarymuseum.org, aka the California State Military Museum, 28th and B streets, Sacramento, CA.

Camp Aliceville—www.encyclopediaofalabama.org/face/Article.isp?id-2322.

Camp Hearne Museum—camphearne.com/index.htm

Camp Opelika—www.eastalabama.org/Exhibits/Exhibits.htm

Camp Roberts Historical Museum—Bldg. 114

Camp Roberts, CA 93451-5000 (12 miles north of Paso Robles, CA) at www.camprobertshistoricalmuseum.com/

Camp Ruston—www.latech.edu/library/scma/index.php

Camp Van Dorn World War II Museum—www.vandorn.org

Cemetery Records Online—www.interment.net

Door County Maritime Museum, Sturgeon Bay, WI has display on WWII POWs in the area orchards

Drew County Museum, Monticello, AR has a display on WWII POWs at Camp Monticello.

Eastern California Museum, Lone Pine, CA at www.inyocounty.us/ecmsite/

Family Search—familysearch.org

Find a Grave—www.findagrave.com

Fort Douglas, Salt Lake City, UT—www.fortdouglas.org/about/virtual-tour, also cemetery

Fort George G. Meade Museum—www.ftmeade.army.mil/museum/Museum_POW.html

Fort Leonard Wood Museum—www.visitmo.com/museums-at-fort-leonard-_wood.aspx

GenTracer—World War II—www.gentracer.org

Library of Congress—catalog.loc.gov

March Field Air Museum, Riverside, CA—www.marchfield.org

Mississippi Armed Forces Museum, Camp Shelby, MS—www.armedforcesmuseum.us/Pages/Newsletter.pdf

Mountain Empire Historical Society and Stone Museum, Campo, CA at www.cssmus.org/

Palm Springs Air Museum, Palm Springs, CA_at palmspringsairmuseum.org/

General George S. Patton Memorial Museum, Chiriaco Summit, CA at generalpattonmuseum.com/

Traces—www.traces.org

Tracy Historical Museum, 1141 Adams St., Tracy, CA

UK National Archives—www.nationalarchives.gov.uk

US Dept. of Veterans Affairs National Cemeteries at www.cem.va.gov/cem/cems/listcem.asp

US National Archives and Records Administration—www.archives.gov

US National Park Service—www.nps.gov

Weber State University, Stewart Library, Special Collections Exhibits, "Prisoners of War in Ogden" at library.weber.edu/collections/special_collections

Bibliography

Adams, Meredith Lentz. "A Miscarriage of Justice?" interview by Jim Kelly. Sunflower Journeys Home 16101A. KTWU. 2003.

Adams, Meredith Lentz. *Murder and Martial Justice: Spying and Retribution in World War II America*. Kent, Ohio: Kent State University Press, 2011.

Adams, Meredith Lentz. "The Abortive Attempt to Exchange GI and German POWs". (Presentation, TRACES conference, 31 May 2003).

Alberts, Betty. Interview by author. 10 March 2012.

Amdt, Karl John Richard. "German P.O.W. Camp Papers." Microfilm. Washington, DC: Library of Congress Photo-duplication Service, 1965. Library of Congress. lccn.loc.gov/83125121.

Angerilli, Adriano. Interview by author. 14 August 2009.

Army Service Forces. "Service Command Operating Personnel and Prisoners, 31 March 1945", NARA RG 389, Entry 261, Box 2563. National Archives at College Park, College Park, MD.

Bischoff, Matt C., *The Desert Training Center/California-Arizona Maneuver Area, 1942-1944: Historical and Archaeological Contexts*. Statistical Research, Inc., 2006

Bland, John Paul. *Secret War at Home: The Pine Grove Furnace Prisoner of War Interrogation Camp*. Cumberland County Historical Society, Carlisle, PA, 2006.

Boudreaux, Henry J, Capt., C.M.P. Report of Investigation of the deaths of Leonello Bini, Vito Clemente, Adolfo Nitri, Antonino Paleologo, 21 July 1943, NARA RG 389, Entry 461, Box 2562. National Archives at College Park, College Park, MD.

Bryan, B.M., Brigadeer General. Assistant Provost Marshal General, Letter to Army Services Forces regarding transfer of POWs, 26 August 1944, NARA RG 389, Entry 457, Box 1419. National Archives at College Park, College Park, MD.

Bulkat, Ernst. Interview by author. 11 March 2007.

Bykofsky, Joseph and Harold Larson. *United States Army in World War II: The Technical Services: The Transportation Corps: Operations Overseas*. Center of Military History, United States Army, Washington, DC, 2003.

California, Death Index, 1940-1997, index, FamilySearch (https://familysearch.org/pal:/MM9.1.1/VPQ6-LWS), Albert Assmann, 1945; citing California Department of Health Services, Vital Statistics Section, Sacramento, CA.

California, Death Index, 1940-1997, index, FamilySearch (https://familysearch.org/pal:/MM9.1.1/VGB7-8K4), Willi Behrens, 1944; citing California Department of Health Services, Vital Statistics Section, Sacramento, CA.

California, Death Index, 1940-1997, index, FamilySearch (https://familysearch.org/pal:/MM9.1.1/VP6Z-CMY), Willi Berkemer, 1945; citing California Department of Health Services, Vital Statistics Section, Sacramento, CA.

California, Death Index, 1940-1997, index, FamilySearch (https://familysearch.org/pal:/MM9.1.1/VG5K-32J), Wilhelm Bethke, 1946; citing California Department of Health Services, Vital Statistics Section, Sacramento, CA.

California, Death Index, 1940-1997, index, FamilySearch (https://familysearch.org/pal:/MM9.1.1/VPQ6-VWW), Renato Boarino, 1945; citing California Department of Health Services, Vital Statistics Section, Sacramento, CA.

California, Death Index, 1940-1997, index, FamilySearch (https://familysearch.org/pal:/MM9.1.1/VPKM-DYZ), Pasquale Carvutto, 1944; citing California Department of Health Services, Vital Statistics Section, Sacramento, CA.

California, Death Index, 1940-1997, index, FamilySearch (https://familysearch.org/pal:/MM9.1.1/VGY8-CT7), Johann Denzel, 1944; citing California Department of Health Services, Vital Statistics Section, Sacramento, CA.

California, Death Index, 1940-1997, index, FamilySearch (https://familysearch.org/pal:/MM9.1.1/VPQV-C9L), Georg Deul, 1946; citing California Department of Health Services, Vital Statistics Section, Sacramento, CA.

California, Death Index, 1940-1997, index, FamilySearch (https://familysearch.org/pal:/MM9.1.1/VP2P-G8Y), Hans Fischer, 1945; citing California Department of Health Services, Vital Statistics Section, Sacramento, CA.

California, Death Index, 1940-1997, index, FamilySearch (https://familysearch.org/pal:/MM9.1.1/VPV1-L2W), Ernst Gall, 1944; citing California Department of Health Services, Vital Statistics Section, Sacramento, CA.

California, Death Index, 1940-1997, index, FamilySearch (https://familysearch.org/pal:/MM9.1.1/VP8X-CZ5), Vito Giardullo, 1944; citing California Department of Health Services, Vital Statistics Section, Sacramento, CA.

California, Death Index, 1940-1997, index, FamilySearch (https://familysearch.org/pal:/MM9.1.1/VG5V-JZ3), Josef Giersberg, 1945; citing California Department of Health Services, Vital Statistics Section, Sacramento, CA.

California, Death Index, 1940-1997, index, FamilySearch (https://familysearch.org/pal:/MM9.1.1/VG5V-B91), Luigi Gori, 1945; citing California Department of Health Services, Vital Statistics Section, Sacramento, CA.

California, Death Index, 1940-1997, index, FamilySearch (https://familysearch.org/pal:/MM9.1.1/VPJC-L2G), Rosario Granata, 1945; citing California Department of Health Services, Vital Statistics Section, Sacramento, CA.

California, Death Index, 1940-1997, index, FamilySearch (https://familysearch.org/pal:/MM9.1.1/VPQX-RJ8), Giovanni Guerrieri, 1945; citing California Department of Health Services, Vital Statistics Section, Sacramento, CA.

California, Death Index, 1940-1997, index, FamilySearch (https://familysearch.org/pal:/MM9.1.1/VP8Q-XCR), Karl Heinz Hafer, 1945; citing California Department of Health Services, Vital Statistics Section, Sacramento, CA.

California, Death Index, 1940-1997, index, FamilySearch (https://familysearch.org/pal:/MM9.1.1/VPQF-7R9), Longin Haussler, 1945; citing California Department of Health Services, Vital Statistics Section, Sacramento, CA.

California, Death Index, 1940-1997, index, FamilySearch (https://familysearch.org/pal:/MM9.1.1/VPQX-BV8), Georg Heinze, 1945; citing California Department of Health Services, Vital Statistics Section, Sacramento, CA.

California, Death Index, 1940-1997, index, FamilySearch (https://familysearch.org/pal:/MM9.1.1/VP81-P8X), Heinz Knopf, 1945; citing California Department of Health Services, Vital Statistics Section, Sacramento, CA.

California, Death Index, 1940-1997, index, FamilySearch (https://familysearch.org/pal:/MM9.1.1/VG52-NY9), Wolfgang Kuerschner, 1946; citing California Department of Health Services, Vital Statistics Section, Sacramento, CA.

California, Death Index, 1940-1997, index, FamilySearch (https://familysearch.org/pal:/MM9.1.1/VPQF-JLV), George Maierhofer, 1945; citing California Department of Health Services, Vital Statistics Section, Sacramento, CA.

California, Death Index, 1940-1997, index, FamilySearch (https://familysearch.org/pal:/MM9.1.1/VGYD-FPK), Richard A Mangold, 1945; citing California Department of Health Services, Vital Statistics Section, Sacramento, CA.

California, Death Index, 1940-1997, index, FamilySearch (https://familysearch.org/pal:/MM9.1.1/VPQK-PQX), Walter Mattick, 1946; citing California Department of Health Services, Vital Statistics Section, Sacramento, CA.

California, Death Index, 1940-1997, index, FamilySearch (https://familysearch.org/pal:/MM9.1.1/VP2J-P2N), Werner Mattner, 1945; citing California Department of Health Services, Vital Statistics Section, Sacramento, CA.

California, Death Index, 1940-1997, index, FamilySearch (https://familysearch.org/pal:/MM9.1.1/VPQF-R94), Richard Neuhaus, 1945; citing California Department of Health Services, Vital Statistics Section, Sacramento, CA.

California, Death Index, 1940-1997, index, FamilySearch (https://familysearch.org/pal:/MM9.1.1/VPQN-9N1), Wilhelm F Oellerich, 1945; citing California Department of Health Services, Vital Statistics Section, Sacramento, CA.

California, Death Index, 1940-1997, index, FamilySearch (https://familysearch.org/pal:/MM9.1.1/VPQF-R4F), Giorgio Palmarini, 1945; citing California Department of Health Services, Vital Statistics Section, Sacramento, CA.

California, Death Index, 1940-1997, index, FamilySearch (https://familysearch.org/pal:/MM9.1.1/VP2K-11W), Vincenzo Pellino, 1944; citing California Department of Health Services, Vital Statistics Section, Sacramento, CA.

California, Death Index, 1940-1997, index, FamilySearch (https://familysearch.org/pal:/MM9.1.1/VG5J-MSF), Angelo Preda, 1944; citing California Department of Health Services, Vital Statistics Section, Sacramento, CA.

California, Death Index, 1940-1997, index, FamilySearch (https://familysearch.org/pal:/MM9.1.1/VPV1-RLQ), Alfredo Prete, 1944; citing California Department of Health Services, Vital Statistics Section, Sacramento, CA.

California, Death Index, 1940-1997, index, FamilySearch (https://familysearch.org/pal:/MM9.1.1/VPQN-NSX), Niccolo Riggi, 1945; citing California Department of Health Services, Vital Statistics Section, Sacramento, CA.

California, Death Index, 1940-1997, index, FamilySearch (https://familysearch.org/pal:/MM9.1.1/VG5J-V47), Tarcisio Riva, 1944; citing California Department of Health Services, Vital Statistics Section, Sacramento, CA.

California, Death Index, 1940-1997, index, FamilySearch (https://familysearch.org/pal:/MM9.1.1/VP8Y-1L1), Luigi Schianta, 1944; citing California Department of Health Services, Vital Statistics Section, Sacramento, CA.

California, Death Index, 1940-1997, index, FamilySearch (https://familysearch.org/pal:/MM9.1.1/VP68-46M), Domenico Schiavo, 1944; citing California Department of Health Services, Vital Statistics Section, Sacramento, CA.

California, Death Index, 1940-1997, index, FamilySearch (https://familysearch.org/pal:/MM9.1.1/VPQJ-QM5), Alfred Stark, 1945; citing California Department of Health Services, Vital Statistics Section, Sacramento, CA.

California, Death Index, 1940-1997, index, FamilySearch (https://familysearch.org/pal:/MM9.1.1/VG5K-NZY), Herbert Vanradecke, 1945; citing California Department of Health Services, Vital Statistics Section, Sacramento, CA.

California, Death Index, 1940-1997, index, FamilySearch (https://familysearch.org/pal:/MM9.1.1/VPQJ-3Y4), Alfred Wagner, 1945; citing California Department of Health Services, Vital Statistics Section, Sacramento, CA.

California State Military Museum, www.militarymuseum.org

Carlson, Lewis. "POW Experience: Myth and Reality". (Presentation, TRACES conference, 6 October 2002).

Conn, Stetson and Byron Fairchild. *The United States Army in World War II, The Western Hemisphere, The Framework of Hemisphere Defense.* Washington, DC: Office of the Chief of Military History, Department of the Army, 1960.

Conn, Stetson and Rose C Engelman and Byron Fairchild, *The United States Army in World War II, The Western Hemisphere, Guarding the United States and its Outposts.* Washington, DC: Office of the Chief of Military History, Department of the Army, 1964

Corbin, Alexander, *The History of Camp Tracy: Japanese WWII POWs and the Future of Strategic Interrogation.* Fort Belvoir, VA: Ziedon Press, 2009

Cosentini, George and Norman Gruenzner. *United States Numbered Military Post Offices Assignments and Locations 1941-1994.* The Military Postal History Society, 1994.

Cowley, Betty. *Stalag Wisconsin: Inside WWII Prisoner-of-war Camps.* Oregon, WI: Badger Books, 2002.

Cunningham, Raymond Kelly. *Prisoners at Fort Douglas: War Prison Barracks Three and the alien enemies, 1917-1920.* Salt Lake City, UT: Fort Douglas Military Museum, 1983.

Daugherty, Joseph B., Col. Assistant, Office of the Quartermaster General, Letter to Provost Marshal General regarding repatriation of ISU units, dated 9 October 1945, NARA RG 389, Entry 261, Box 2563. National Archives and Records Administration, College Park, MD

Daugherty, Joseph B., Col. Assistant, Office of the Quartermaster General, Letter to Provost Marshal General regarding repatriation of ISU units, dated 28 August 1945, NARA RG 389, Entry 261, Box 2563. National Archives and Records Administration, College Park, MD

"Department of Veterans Affairs National Cemeteries," United States Department of Veterans Affairs, www.cem.va.gov/cem/cems/listcem.asp.

Ducharme, Joseph O.C., Lt. Col. Director, Enemy PW Information Bureau, Camp Holabird, MD, to Provost Marshal General, regarding cemetery locations, dated 16 February 1953, NARA RG 389, Entry 261, Box 2562. National Archives and Records Administration, College Park, MD

Ducharme, Joseph O.C., Lt. Col. Director, Enemy PW Information Bureau, Camp Holabird, MD, to Provost Marshal General, Regarding cemetery locations, dated 16 February 1953, NARA RG 389, Entry 467, Box 1513. National Archives and Records Administration, College Park, MD

Dvorak, Petula. "Fort Hunt's Quiet Men Break Silence on WWII: Interrogator Fought "Battle of Wits."" *The Washington Post.* 6 October 2007.

Edwards, Earl L., Lt. Col. Asst. Dir., Prisoner of War Division, Letter to Army Services Forces, regarding prisoner segregation, dated 3 March 1944, NARA RG 389, Entry 261, Box 2563. National Archives and Records Administration, College Park, MD

Edwards, Earl L., Lt. Col. Asst. Dir., Prisoner of War Division, Letter Regarding Prisoner Transfer, dated 16 October 1943, NARA RG 389, Entry 261, Box 2563. National Archives and Records Administration, College Park, MD

Edwards, Earl L., Lt. Col. Asst. Dir., Prisoner of War Division, Letter Regarding Prisoner Transfer, dated 7 January 1943, NARA RG 389, Entry 261, Box 2563. National Archives and Records Administration, College Park, MD

Enemy Prisoner of War Information Bureau. "World War II Enemy Prisoners of War Deceased in Theaters of Operations, Fort Holabird, MD, 2 July 1952", NARA RG 389, Entry 466, Box 1. National Archives and Records Administration, College Park, MD

Eppinga, Jane. *Death at Papago Park POW Camp: A Tragic Murder and America's Last Mass Execution.* Charleston, SC: The History Press, 2017.

Erichsen, Heino R. *The Reluctant Warrior: Former German POW Finds Peace in Texas.* Austin, TX: Eakin Press, 2001.

Erichsen, Heino R. Interview by author. 7 October 2002.

Fairchild, Byron and Jonathan Grossman. *United States Army in World War II: The War Department: The Army and Industrial Manpower.* Center of Military History, Department of the Army, Washington, DC, 2002.

Farrand, Stephen M. Major, Prisoner of War Operations Division, Letter to Special War Problems Division regarding the death of Karl Schaeffer, dated 28 May 1945, NARA RG 389, Entry 261, Box 2562. National Archives and Records Administration, College Park, MD

Farrand, Stephen M. Major, Prisoner of War Operations Division, Letter to Special War Problems Division regarding the death of Alfred Malinowski, dated 20 February 1945, NARA RG 389, Entry 261, Box 2562. National Archives and Records Administration, College Park, MD

"Find a Grave," Find a Grave, www.findagrave.com/.

Fischer, H.P., Office of the Commanding General, Ninth Service Command, Fort Douglas, UT, Letter to Army Service Forces regarding new base camps, dated 31 March 1945, NARA RG 389, Entry 457, Box 1419. National Archives and Records Administration, College Park, MD

Ford, George. "German Guard Held in Medical Ward After Shooting 28 Germans: Probe Opened by Army Into Salina Affair". The Deseret News, 9 July 1945.

Gansberg, Judith M., *Stalag: USA: The Remarkable Story of German POWs in America.* New York, NY: Thomas Y. Crowell Company, 1977.

Geiger, Jeffrey, *The German Prisoners of War at Camp Cooke*, Jefferson, NC: McFarland & Company, Inc., 1996

Giordana, Beth. Interview by author. August 2001.

Griffith, L.E. Lt. Col., Prisoner of War Operations Division, Letter to Mrs. Ada Errera regarding transfer of body to Italy, dated 30 April 1946, NARA RG 389, Entry 261, Box 2562. National Archives and Records Administration, College Park, MD

Hamann, Jack. *On American Soil: How Justice Became a Casualty of World War II.* Algonquin Books, 2005.

Heisler, Barbara Schmitter. "Returning to America: German Prisoners of War and the American Experience", German Studies Review, Vol. 31, No. 3 (Oct., 2008), pp. 537-556; Published by: The Johns Hopkins University Press on behalf of the German Studies Association

Heitmann, John A. "Enemies are Human." (Presentation, Dayton Christian-Jewish Dialogue, 10 May 1998).

Iannantuoni, Mario. Interview by author. 10 February 2012.

Jensen, Carol A. *Images of America: Byron Hot Springs*. San Francisco, CA: Arcadia Publishing, 2006.

Jones, L.B.C. Lt. Col. Deputy Director, Internal Security Division, Regarding Security, dated 14 October 1943, NARA RG 389, Entry 261, Box 2563. National Archives and Records Administration, College Park, MD

Keefer, Louis E., *Italian Prisoners of War in America, 1942-1946: Captives or Allies?* New York, NY: Praeger, 1992.

Kirkpatrick, Kathy. "Italian POWs in Utah." (Presentation, TRACES conference, 7 October 2002)

Kirkpatrick, Kathy. (Presentation, TRACES conference 31 May 2003).

Kleinman, Steven M. "The History of MIS-Y: US Strategic Interrogation During World War II". Master's thesis, Joint Military Intelligence College, 2002.

Knappe, Siegfried & Ted Brusaw. *Soldat: Reflections of a German Soldier 1936-1949.* New York, NY: Orion Books, 1992.

Krammer, Arnold. "American Treatment of German Generals" The Journal of Military History 54, No. 1 (January 1990): 27-46.

Krammer, Arnold. "German Prisoners of War in the United States" Military Affairs 40, No. 2 (April 1976): 68-73.

Krammer, Arnold. *Nazi Prisoners of War in America.* Lanham, MD: Scarborough House, 1996.

Leighton, Richard M., and Robert W. Coakley. *The United States Army in World War II, The War Department, Global Logistics and Strategy 1940-1943*, Washington, DC: Office of the Chief of Military History, Department of the Army, 1955.

Lewis, George G, and John Mewha. *History of Prisoner of War Utilization by the United States Army, 1776-1945.* US Department of the Army, Pamphlet 20-213, Washington, DC: Government Printing Office, 1955.

L'Ufficio Informazione Vaticano per I pregionieri di guerra istituito da Pio XII, Vatican Secret Archives. Vatican City.

Lucioli, Ezio. Interview by author. 14 August 2009.

Luick-Thrams, Michael. "The Fritz Ritz: German POWs in the American Heartland" (Presentation, TRACES conference, 31 May 2003).

Margotilli, Giuseppe. Interview by author. 14 August 2009.

Martin, Charles E., Col., Director of Personnel, Memorandum to Armed Service Forces, regarding release of ISU, dated 3 October 1945, NARA RG 389, Entry 261, Box 2563. National Archives and Records Administration, College Park, MD

Martin, Charles E., Col., Director of Personnel, Memorandum to Armed Service Forces, regarding release of ISU, dated 23 August 1945, NARA RG 389, Entry 261, Box 2563. National Archives and Records Administration, College Park, MD

Martin, Charles E., Col., Director of Personnel, Memorandum to Armed Service Forces, regarding release of ISU, dated 20 August 1945, NARA RG 389, Entry 261, Box 2563. National Archives and Records Administration, College Park, MD

Meier, Susan Ann, "Limited Freedom: The Italian Service Units in Southern California's Inland Empire During World War II". Thesis at California State University, Fullerton: 2004

Moore, John Hammond. "Italian POWs in America: War is Not Always Hell." Prologue (Fall 1976): 141-151.

Moore, John Hammond. *Wacko War: Strange Tales from America 1941-1945.* Raleigh, NC: Pentland Press, 2001.

Nagler, Joerg A. "Enemy Aliens and Internment in World War I: Alvo von Alvensleben in Fort Douglas, Utah, a Case Study." Utah Historical Quarterly 58 (Fall 1990): 388-406

Nash, Gerald D. *The American West Transformed: The Impact of the Second World War.* Bloomington, IN: Indiana University Press, 1985.

National Archives and Records Administration, Record Group 38. Records of the Navy; Special Activities Branch (OP-16-Z), Navy Unit, Tracy, California. National Archives and Records Administration, College Park, MD

National Archives and Records Administration, Record Group 331. Records of Allied Operational and Occupation Headquarters, World War II. Entry 3A, Box 126. Repatriation to USSR. National Archives and Records Administration, College Park, MD

National Archives and Records Administration, Record Group 389. Records of the Office of the Provost Marshal General. National Archives and Records Administration, College Park, MD

Orsini, August. Interview by author. 7 October 2011.

Palermo, Raffaele. "ISU Personnel Records." Al Ministero della Difesa, Rome, Italy.

Parri, Dino. *Il Giuramento; Generale a El Alamein, prigioniero in America (1942-1945).* Milano: Mursia, 2009.

"Per il Soldato Francesco Erriquez la guerra è finita!" Un Mondo di Italiani, www.unmondoditaliani.com/per-il-soldato-francesco-erriquez-la-guerra-e-finita.htm.

Pisani, Pat and Maria. Interview by author. 12 June 2009.

Powell, Allan Kent. *Splinters of a Nation; German Prisoners of War in Utah.* Salt Lake City, UT: University of Utah Press, 1989.

Prisoners in Paradise, DVD, directed by Camilla Calamandrei. 2001.

"Prisoners of War in Ogden: 1943-1946," Weber State University Stewart Library, ibrary.weber.edu/asc/POW/default.cfm.

Pulia, Peter A., Sr. Interview by author. 1 May 2002.

Reiss, Matthias. "Bronzed Bodies behind Barbed Wire: Masculinity and the Treatment of German Prisoners of War in the United States during World War II." The Journal of Military History 69, No. 2 (April 2005): 475-504.

Richards, Su. Interview by author. 23 May 2009.

Rogers, John R. Interview by author. 3 September 2007.

Salgado, Rebecca C. "Rebuilding the Network: Interpretation of World War II Prisoner-of-War Camps in the United States." Master's Thesis, Columbia University, May 2012.

Scott, Ralph. "Violations of International Law in the Treatment of German POWs Following the Cessation of Hostilities". (Presentation, TRACES conference, 1 June 2003).

Smith, Clarence McKittrick. *United States Army in World War II: The Technical Services: The Medical Department: Hospitalization and Evacuation, Zone of Interior.* Center of Military History, United States Army, Washington, DC, 2003.

Spidle, Jake W. Jr. "Axis Prisoners of War in the United States, 1942-1946: A Bibliographical Essay." Military Affairs 39, No. 2 (April 1975): 61-66.

"State Department-Related Sites: Hotels and Resorts," German American Internee Coalition, www.gaic.info/ShowPage.php?section=Internment_Camps_

Storm, Ralph A., *Camp Florence Days.* N.p. 2007.

Thomas, Jennie M. "History of the Prisoner of War Camp Utah ASF Depot, Ogden, UT", 1 February 1945.

Thompson, Antonio S., *Men in German Uniform: POWs in America during World War II.* Knoxville, TN: University of Tennessee Press, 2010.

Tissing, Robert Warren Jr. "Utilization of Prisoners of War in the United States During World War II: Texas, A Case Study". Master's Thesis, Baylor University, 1973.

Todaro, Robert J. Interview by author. 12 June 2006.

Togni, Fernando. Interview by author. 14 August 2009.

Tollefson, A.M., Col., Director, Prisoner of War Operations, Letter to Special Projects Division regarding the death of Giovanni Cincotta, dated 10 January 1946, NARA RG 389, Entry 462, Box 2562. National Archives and Records Administration, College Park, MD

Tollefson, A.M., Col., Director, Prisoner of War Operations, Letter to Special Projects Division regarding the death of Giovanni E. Bondini, dated 8 June 1945, NARA RG 389, Entry 261, Box 2562. National Archives and Records Administration, College Park, MD

Tollefson, A.M., Col., Director, Prisoner of War Operations, Letter to Special Projects Division regarding Salina shooting, dated 28 August 1945, NARA RG 389, Entry 261, Box 2562. National Archives and Records Administration, College Park, MD

Trezzani, Claudio. Letter from Monticello PW Camp, AR, dated 26 January 1944. Stato Maggiore Esercito, No. 2256A, Rome, Italy

Ulio, J.A., Major General, the Adjutant General's office, letter to The Commanding Generals, dated 9 April 1943. NARA RG 389, Entry 261, Box 2563. National Archives and Records Administration, College Park, MD

University of Utah. *Historic Fort Douglas at the University of Utah, a Brief History & Walking Tour.* Salt Lake City, UT: University of Utah, 2000.

Urwiller, Clifford S., Col. Prisoner of War Operations Division, Memorandum for Camp Operations Branch regarding surplus ISU units, dated 18 October 1945, NARA RG 389, Entry 261, Box 2563. National Archives and Records Administration, College Park, MD

Urwiller, Clifford S., Col. Prisoner of War Operations Division, Memorandum for Camp Operations Branch regarding surplus ISU units, dated 14 September 1945, NARA RG 389, Entry 261, Box 2563. National Archives and Records Administration, College Park, MD

US House. Report of Committee on Military Affairs. 78th Congress., 2nd sess., H. Res. 30.

US House. Report of Committee on Military Affairs. 79th Congress., 1st sess., H. Res. 20.

War Department, to Commanding Generals, Regarding movement orders, dated 14 November 1945, NARA RG 389, Entry 261, Box 2563. National Archives and Records Administration, College Park, MD

War Department, to Commanding Generals, Regarding movement orders, dated 1 November 1945, NARA RG 389, Entry 261, Box 2563. National Archives and Records Administration, College Park, MD

War Department, to Commanding Generals, Regarding movement orders, dated 23 October 1945, NARA RG 389, Entry 261, Box 2563. National Archives and Records Administration, College Park, MD

War Department, to Commanding Generals, Regarding movement orders, dated 18 September 1945, NARA RG 389, Entry 261, Box 2563. National Archives and Records Administration, College Park, MD

Wardlow, Chester. *United States Army in World War II: The Technical Services: The Transportation Corps: Movements, Training, and Supply*. Center of Military History, United States Army, Washington, DC, 2003.

Weyand, A.M., Col. Commanding, Prisoner of War Camp, Ogden, UT, Letter regarding prisoner segregation, dated 21 January 1944, NARA RG 389, Entry 261, Box 2563. National Archives and Records Administration, College Park, MD

Whittingham, Richard. *Martial Justice: The Last Mass Execution in the United States*. Bluejacket Books, Naval Institute Press, Annapolis, MD. 1997

Wilcox, Walter W. "The Wartime Use of Manpower on Farms." Journal of Farm Economics 28, No. 3 (Aug. 1946): 723-741.

Winter, Richard. "Hot Springs, NC. A World War I Internment Camp." *North Carolina Postal Historian* 27, no. 1 (2008)

"WWI German Prisoners of War in Utah," GenTracer, www.gentracer.org/WWIGermanPrisonersofWarinUtah.html.

"WWI Internment Camp in Hot Springs, NC: The German Village," Welcome to Madison County, North Carolina, www.visitmadisoncounty.com/who-we-are/town-of-hot-springs/the-german-village-wwi-internment-camp/.

Acknowledgments

Christine Saffell (researcher and travel companion)
Kate and John Saffell (website, data entry, photos)
Alessandro de Gaetano (producer, screenwriter of Red Gold)
Barbara Harvey (Mother, support, great memory for events in her lifetime, AZ)
Carol A. Jensen (historian and author)
Dave Kendziura (historian, Hill AFB, Clearfield, UT)
Gina McNeeley (photographic expert, NARA researcher)
Jinger La Guardia (colleague who shares the goal of saving these "lost" stories)
Karen Jensen and Pam Frisbie (my sisters who share the lure of the stories behind the headstones)
Karrie and Jenefer Jackson (data entry)
Kenneth D. Schlessinger (NARA II, College Park, MD)
Kent Powell (Utah Historical Society, Salt Lake City, UT)
Col. Maurizio Parri (grandson of General Dino Parri, an Italian POW at Camp Monticello, AR)
Michael Luick-Thrams (TRACES founder, IA)
Michael Pomeroy (authority on Camp Monticello, AR)
Mona Daniels (Bureau of Land Management, Needles, CA)
Rhonda Jackson and Lucia Rogers (researchers, AZ)
Sarah Langsdon (Special Collections, Weber State University, Ogden, UT)
Stefano Palermo (son of Raffaele Palermo, an Italian POW in California and Arizona)
Su Richards (historian, Ft. Douglas Museum, Salt Lake City, UT)

Please contact the author at gentracer@gmail.com to share your knowledge about the Prisoners of War stories, photos, letters, and artifacts that may be part of your family and local history.

Alphabetical Index